IS THIS ALL THERE IS?

IS THIS ALL THERE IS?

And Other Big Questions about God and Life

Andy Langford & Mark Ralls

Abingdon Press / Nashville

IS THIS ALL THERE IS?
AND OTHER BIG QUESTIONS ABOUT GOD AND LIFE

Copyright © 2009 by Abingdon Press

This book is printed on acid-free paper.

Library of Congress Cataloging-in-Publication Data

Langford, Andy.
 Is this all there is? : and other big questions about God and life / Andy Langford and Mark Ralls.
    p. cm.
 Rev. ed. of: Beginnings. c2003.
 Includes bibliographical references and index.
 ISBN 978-1-4267-0039-2 (binding: pbk.,/trade : alk. paper)
 1. Christianity—Essence, genius, nature—Miscellanea. 2. Christian life—Miscellanea. I. Ralls, Mark. II. Langford, Andy. Beginnings. III. Title.
 BT60.L38 2009
 230—dc22

                                                                    2008053689

Is This All There Is? And Other Big Questions about God and Life is a revised edition of *Beginnings: An Introduction to Christian Faith (Along the Way)* © 2003 Abingdon Press.

09 10 11 12 13 14 15 16 17 18 — 10 9 8 7 6 5 4 3 2 1

MANUFACTURED IN THE UNITED STATES OF AMERICA

Contents

Introduction

In Lewis Carroll's *Alice's Adventures in Wonderland*, Alice meets the Cheshire Cat sitting in a tree. Alice begins her conversation with the Cat this way:

"Would you tell me, please, which way I ought to walk from here?"

"That depends a good deal on where you want to get to," said the Cat.

"I don't much care where," said Alice.

"Then it doesn't matter which way you walk," said the Cat.

As we shall see, the earliest Christian believers referred to themselves as people of "the Way." Perhaps they meant by this title that they possessed a clear goal and walked a particular path. Those first followers longed to be like Jesus. To follow Jesus was their goal. So they became followers of his way.

In this little book, we invite you to consider some of the questions that seekers often ask about Jesus: Who is Jesus and Why Should I Care? Can I Trust God? How Does God Speak to Me? and How Do I Speak to God? We wrote this book not because we believe we have found all the answers but because we are convinced that the questions themselves have much to teach us. Picture these questions as trail markers gently nudging us forward on a circuitous hike rather than crisp and clear highway signs spelling it all out for us.

Regardless of where we find ourselves along the path, these questions remain. They are never fully resolved and that is part of their peculiar power. These questions lead us forward. They beckon us simply to take the next step in the way of Jesus. We invite you to join us as we travel together.

One

SO, IS THIS ALL THERE IS?

Human being are not born once and for all on the day their mothers give birth to them, but...life obliges them over and over to give birth to themselves midway along the journey of life.

                                        Gabriel Garcia Marquez

Now there was a Pharisee, a man named Nicodemus who was a member of the Jewish ruling council. Nicodemus came to Jesus at night and said, "Rabbi, we know you are a teacher who has come from God. For no one could perform the miraculous signs you are doing if God were not with them" (John 3:1-3a; author's translation).

In the earliest days of the church, Christians were sometimes referred to as the people of "the Way" (Acts 9:2). Their neighbors who called them this were no doubt befuddled by the strange practices of this little band of believers. Yet, one thing was clear: They were bound together by their shared conviction that they had finally found the one thing that gave their lives meaning. As followers of Jesus Christ, they had embarked upon a new way of life that offered them a definite sense of purpose.

Novelist Walker Percy once said that the most important difference in people is between those for whom life is a quest and those for whom it is not. If you are searching for that one thing in life, then this book is an invitation to begin a quest of your own and join us as we explore together the way of Jesus Christ. Ours will be a journey of exploration, a path of inquiry into Christian beliefs and practices. In the end, we hope you will discover something new about Jesus Christ and those who follow him. You may even discover something new about yourself. Some journeys we choose; others choose us. On this journey of discovery, you might find that you have already been discovered by God.

QUESTIONS

A philosopher once said that to become wise, we must learn to ask the questions we asked as a child—simple, direct questions that get right to the heart of the matter. Peggy Lee in 1969 recorded a song about such questions. In the song, when she was twelve, her father took her to the circus, which should have been a very happy occasion for a child. But, as she watched, she felt an emptiness—"Is that all there is?" she asked.

You may be reading this book because you have taken a long, hard look at your life and asked yourself the simple question, "Is this all there is?"

In the Bible, we learn about a man named Nicodemus who also struggled with this question. He was a spiritual person, but he felt that something was still missing. Late one night, Nicodemus came to see Jesus and said, "Teacher, you must tell me. Is this all there is to life? There has to be something more than what I have experienced so far." Jesus answered, in essence, "If you want a new life, you've got to begin again at the very beginning. You've got to start out on a brand new way."

Many of us are haunted by the sense that there must be something more to life, something more lasting, something more substantial than what typically occupies our attention. We long for a life that is rich with meaning and full of purpose. If this longing remains unfulfilled, we carry around the gnawing suspicion that something is missing. Of course, with all the different varieties of coffee, dozens of all-sports cable channels, and an infinitely expanding Internet, there is plenty to distract us from our uncomfortable feeling. Hopping from one experience to the next works—but only for a while. Our hunger remains for that one thing that gives life meaning and purpose. That is why many of us can relate to Nicodemus, who brought a simple, direct question to Jesus and left wondering what it would mean to begin again on a brand new way.

For a brief period near the end of his life, Albert Camus, the great philosopher—assumed to be an atheist—attended a small Methodist church in France. In conversations with his pastor, Camus had this to say about his own search: "This man Nicodemus! . . . He is seeking something that he does not have. I feel right at home with Nicodemus, because I too am uncertain about this whole matter of Christianity. . . . The reason I have been coming to church is because I am seeking. I'm almost on a pilgrimage—seeking something to fill the void I am experiencing. . . . I am searching for something that the world is not giving me."

At times, the search becomes more intense. It may be when a relationship dissolves, when a child is born, or when we decide to get married. It could also be the time when we begin to see through the things that once meant so much to us. Charlie Gray, the hard-driven young banker in John Marquand's *Point of No Return*, relentlessly pursues his goal to become vice president of a prestigious New York bank. Yet, when Charlie reaches this goal, he experiences an unexpected moment: He realizes that this is not what he wanted after all.

No matter how much we get or what we achieve, sooner or later we want something more. We often feel like containers into which things are constantly being poured, but for some reason we never feel full. An ancient preacher in the Bible named Jeremiah said that we are like "cracked cisterns that can hold no water" (Jeremiah 2:13). It is as if there is a hole left vacant within us. Something is always leaking out, and we continually need more and more to be satisfied.

More of the same will not help, however. We need something beyond our experience. For Augustine, a Christian leader of the fourth century, the solution was clear. Our hearts will be "forever restless," he said, "until they rest in [God]." Inside each of us is a void that only God can fill. So we are dissatisfied with all substitutes. We remain unfulfilled until we find the source of our true fulfillment.

A WORLD OF STRANGERS

"In our world full of strangers, estranged from . . . friends and family, from their deepest self and their God, we witness a painful search for a hospitable place where life can be lived . . . and community can be found."

Henri Nouwen

What makes the search for meaning so difficult is that we often feel alone in the process. This is a reflection of our lives. Several writers have commented in recent years on the rapid changes in our culture. William Leach, for instance, notes what he describes as the "destruction of place in American life." He says that our lives are increasingly defined by temporary things: temporary homes, temporary jobs, temporary vehicles, temporary mates. We are gradually losing our ties to the people and places that used to help us secure meaning. We see this in a hundred little ways. Compared to past generations, we work more hours with longer commutes. We shop in sprawling super centers rather than in corner markets where neighbor mingles with neighbor. We communicate through e-mail rather than face-to-face. We eat take-out in front of the television rather than around a table with friends or family. All of these little losses of community add up to leave us feeling depleted and displaced. We experience loneliness in a variety of forms: a vague "dis-ease," a deep dissatisfaction, a persistent longing for real connection.

In Walker Percy's novel *The Gramercy Winner*, we witness a conversation between Will Grey and his psychologist, Dr. Scanlon:

"What's the matter, Willy?"

"I don't know, Scanlon. I'm homesick."

"How long have you been homesick?"

"All my life."

"Let me seek thee in my desire, let me desire thee in my seeking. Let me find thee by loving thee, let me love thee when I find thee."   *Anselm of Canterbury*

Perhaps you have found yourself continuously searching for "that one thing" that will allow you to feel at home, the missing key that finally turns the lock, the elusive piece of the puzzle that makes it all come together. If you are asking the simple question "Is this all there is?" you are bumping your head against a mystery. Is there more to life than we can measure? Is there more to this world than we know? You may sense that there is nothing in our human experience that completely fills the needs of your heart. You might find yourself looking beyond the borders of what this life has to offer. This is no cause for concern. Some journeys end precisely where a new one begins.

Two

WHO IS JESUS, AND WHY SHOULD I CARE?

Jesus came to reunite, to heal, to form bonds, to reconcile.
Henri Nouwen

[Jesus] left Judea and went back once more to Galilee.

Now he had to go through Samaria. So he came to a town in Samaria called Sychar…and Jesus, tired as he was from the journey, sat down by the well. It was about the sixth hour [noon].

When a Samaritan woman came to draw water, Jesus said to her, "Will you give me a drink?"…

The Samaritan woman said to him, "You are a Jew and I am a Samaritan woman. How can you ask me for a drink?" (For Jews do not associate with Samaritans.)

Jesus answered her, "If you knew the gift of God and who it is that asks you for a drink, you would have asked him and he would have given you living water."

"Sir," the woman said, "you have nothing to draw with and the well is deep. Where can you get this living water?"…

Jesus answered, "Everyone who drinks this water will be thirsty again, but whoever drinks the water I give him will never thirst. Indeed, the water I give him will become in him a spring of water welling up to eternal life."

The woman said to him, "Sir, give me this water so that I won't get thirsty and have to keep coming here to draw water...."

Jesus declared, "Believe me, woman, a time is coming when you will worship the Father neither on this mountain nor in Jerusalem...."

The woman said, "I know that Messiah" (called Christ) "is coming. When he comes, he will explain everything to us."

Then Jesus declared, "I who speak to you am he...."

Then, leaving her water jar, the woman went back to the town and said to the people, "Come, see a man who told me everything I ever did. Could this be the Christ?" (John 4:3-29 NIV)

Who was Jesus? Was he a practical teacher? A social revolutionary? An ancient magician? Here is how Thomas Cahill, a contemporary historian, answers this question:

"Two thousand years ago a man was born into a family of carpenters in occupied Palestine. He was a small-town Jew. ...He preached a message of mercy, love and peace and was crucified for his trouble. This unlikely character has long been accounted the central figure of Western civilization. Even now...we count our days by his appearance on earth; and, though our supposedly post-Christian society often ignores and even ridicules him, there are no serious suggestions for replacing him as the Icon of the West."

Most people hold Jesus in high esteem. Almost everyone considers Jesus a great religious leader, someone comparable to the Buddha, Mohammed, or Confucius. Without discounting the contributions of these and other great spiritual teachers, Christians believe Jesus is unique. We believe that in this person God became present to human beings in a completely new way, that this man from a town called Nazareth allows us to see clearly the true nature of God. We also believe that if we recognize Jesus of Nazareth for who he really is, we will want to follow him. We believe that by modeling ourselves after his life and teachings, we will discover the meaning and purpose of our own lives. This commitment to follow Jesus Christ is what it means to describe ourselves as Christians.

JESUS AS THE SON OF GOD

For many people Christmas is the happiest time of the year. As Christmas cards express it, Christmas is a season of "good cheer" spent with family and close friends. Christmas cards also remind us of the familiar cast of characters who started it all: Mary, Joseph, and the baby—lined up in front of a stable full of straw and animals. Regardless of how we understand the story of Jesus' birth, Christmas evokes in us noble, life-affirming qualities like peace, joy, and love (Luke 2:1-20). During the Christmas season, we may become acutely aware of a yearning to find a deeper purpose, a more substantial truth, in our lives.

Yet, for Christians, the meaning of Christmas goes beyond the awareness of spiritual yearning. Because we believe that the desire for all the truly good things of life is connected to our longing for God, Christmas also commemorates what God did to satisfy our deepest desires.

For us, Jesus' coming into the world is a love story. It is not only about the love shared by Joseph and Mary but also about God's love for all humanity. The moral of the story of Jesus' birth is found in one of the most popular lines of the Bible, John 3:16: "For God so loved the world that he gave his only Son." Christmas reminds us that God is so passionately in love with us that God gives us something of God's own self. At the first Christmas, God became present to us as a helpless baby born in a humble stable. No longer is God far off in some heavenly realm. God came "down here" to be with us. Christmas tells a love story beyond our wildest dreams. In the midst of our desperate search for God, God came along and found us.

Christians describe this incredible event as the Incarnation of God. *Incarnation* is not a word that comes up every day. Yet, if we break the word apart, the idea behind incarnation is not so difficult to understand. The Latin root, *carne*, means "flesh." So *in-carne* means to be "in-fleshed" or embodied. Jesus of Nazareth, we believe, is God-in-the-flesh. All that God is became focused in this particular human being. The mysterious, unseen God was revealed as Jesus, a person who could be seen, touched, and known.

God was not disguised as a human being in the way Superman would disguise himself as Clark Kent. When we call Jesus the Son of God, we mean that he actually was God-in-the-flesh. This may seem strange; but think of it this way: When students are confused by some difficult idea, they might ask their teacher, "Could you flesh that out for us?" What they mean is that they need an example to make it clearer and easier to grasp. This is what Jesus does for us. He is the concrete example of God's love. He helps us see God more clearly. In him the mystery of God is "fleshed out" for us.

> *"God ... became human...was born into the world as an actual man....If you want to get the hang of it, think of how you would like to become a slug or a crab."*
>
> C. S. Lewis

Exactly how the Incarnation happened is impossible to understand, but it might be analogous to a phenomenon in art. Sometimes an artist paints one picture on a canvas—say, a portrait—then later reuses the canvas, painting a landscape or a still life over the original image. As the top layer of paint fades over time, the earlier lines and colors of the portrait may bleed through. This subtle effect can be haunting. A bowl of fruit mysteriously appears in the middle of a field of horses; a brilliant sunset shines through a woman's face. When Christians say that Jesus was the incarnation of God, we are suggesting that something like this happened in Jesus' life. Somehow the true nature of God shone through him. When we encounter Jesus Christ, we see the faint outline of our Creator. This is something of what Christians mean when we call Jesus the Son of God.

The Incarnation, however, is just the beginning of the story. What actually happened when the very nature of God became expressed in the life of one particular person? We find our answer in the first four books of the New Testament—Matthew, Mark, Luke, and John. These books provide four separate accounts of the life of Jesus, depicting him as a healer, as a teacher, and, ultimately, as Messiah.

JESUS AS HEALER

Little is known about Jesus' youth. Most likely, he worked with Joseph, his father, a carpenter in Nazareth.

We can imagine that Jesus spent his days working with his hands and his evenings studying Jewish teachings late into the night. How else could he have astounded a group of rabbis with his wisdom when he was only twelve (Luke 2:41-50)? He must have also spent many hours in prayer because it gradually became clear to him that God had a special purpose for his life—a mission that would be like none before or since.

When he was about thirty years old, Jesus stood before the synagogue in Nazareth and announced what this mission would be: "God's Spirit is on me.... [God has] sent me to announce pardon to prisoners and recovery of sight to the blind, To set the burdened and battered free, to announce, 'This is God's year to act!' " (Luke 4:18-19 *The Message*).

Wherever Jesus went, people were transformed by his presence. When people found out that Jesus had unusual healing power, they flocked to him; and, indeed, he performed great miracles. Some were cured of physical ailments such as blindness and paralysis. Many more were freed from emotional problems. When the question was raised whether Jesus was truly sent by God, he would typically respond, by pointing not to his incredible powers but to what was happening in the lives of people he encountered.

One of the people Jesus healed was a man with leprosy. In Jesus' day, a leper was treated as an outcast as was anyone who touched a leper, even by accident. According to religious law, lepers were required to cover their mouths and cry out, "Unclean, unclean!" whenever they were in public. People recoiled in horror at the sight of lepers.

Jesus, however, had the opposite reaction. We are told that when Jesus encountered a leper, he was "moved with pity," that he reached out his hand and touched one who was "untouchable." The man was immediately cured. He was also restored in a deeper sense, finding acceptance in Jesus who responded to him not in horror, but with compassion (Mark 1:40-45).

One of the most distinguishing characteristics of Jesus was the way he accepted people. This, too, was a kind of healing, especially in an ancient society that operated on a strict caste system in which some people were simply not acceptable. Jesus welcomed one and all. He seemed to enjoy nothing more than a festive dinner with good friends. This included poor fishermen, prostitutes, beggars, crooked tax collectors, the poor, and the sick. Jesus had a remarkable ability to make these "lost" people feel comfortable in his presence. With the invitation "Come unto me all you...who are weighed down with burdens" (Matthew 11:28; author's translation), Jesus welcomed the most unacceptable people of his day and left them transformed by his friendship.

One of the persons Jesus healed in this way was a woman from the neighboring region of Samaria (John 4:1-42). She was shocked when Jesus approached her and asked for a drink of water. In the caste system of Jesus' day, Jews considered Samaritans to be untouchable. In that day, a Jewish person like Jesus would never talk with someone from Samaria. Jesus saw something more than a political enemy; he saw into the deep desires of her heart. He told her things about herself that no stranger could have known. For instance, Jesus pointed out that she had been married five times and that the man she was now with was not her husband. While this may seem like an insensitive thing to say, Jesus was actually saying that he knew the depth of her pain. In those days women were considered the property of their husbands. That she had been married so many times undoubtedly meant that she had been terribly mistreated. She had been taken advantage of by a society that was often cruel to women. Passed from man to man, she no longer even had the dignity of marriage, so crucial in her day. Jesus noticed the injustice of her situation, and he addressed it with compassion.

In response, this woman could sense something remarkable about Jesus. She wondered if he might be the Son of God and asked everyone she knew, "Could this be the Christ?" Jesus healed her by offering her the dignity and acceptance that she had never before experienced.

When we say that Jesus was a healer, we are not referring simply to the miracles he performed. We mean that Jesus' life was pure and complete in a way that the world had never seen before. When people encountered such wholeness, they saw the way life was meant to be lived. They became aware that something was missing from their lives, and they sensed that this void could somehow be filled by following the one who had cured them.

It is said that some Native Americans would revere a special group of "contrary people" whose role was to do the opposite of what everyone else was doing. Their behavior would challenge the tribe's notion of how things ought to be. In a sense, this is what Jesus did. He cut against the grain of the most cherished assumptions of his day, and in so doing he offered people a way out of their brokenness—a living water that would satisfy them once and for all. In this way Jesus not only healed but also was a healer.

JESUS AS TEACHER

"This man-God Jesus was a good story teller. He knew what he was doing."   Lois Cheney

Think back about your teachers. Can you remember an English teacher whose passion for poetry stirred your own? Can you recall a high school coach who pushed and leaned hard on you because he or she seemed almost desperate for you to reach your potential? Can you remember a calculus professor who spent hour after hour with you until equations were more than just numbers on a page, and you suddenly grasped the beauty of mathematics? Great teachers do far more than convey information. Great teachers inspire us. They propel us forward by opening up a new world of understanding.

This was the kind of teacher Jesus was. When Jesus taught—in the open air along country roads, on hillsides, and beside lakeshores—he always attracted a crowd. To the people who came to hear him, what he taught was unlike anything they had encountered—and yet his teaching rang true. Speaking in riddles, parables, and unexpected paradoxes, Jesus turned people's assumptions upside down. He often began with the words, "You have heard that it was said…" followed by a familiar assumption—only to challenge that perspective with the words, "But I say to you…" offering a brand new way of approaching life (for instance, Matthew 5:21-22). Something about who he was and the way he taught touched people to the very core of their lives and challenged them to begin a whole new way of life.

Jesus' message was simple. God's love is absolute, and we are meant to reflect that love in every aspect of our lives. This is our purpose in life, and the first step toward realizing it is to see the radical, unexpected way that God loves each of us. Jesus portrayed this mystery in a variety of ways, but perhaps his favorite was through stories. In one story he portrayed God as a heartsick father who ran out to welcome his wayward, rebellious son (Luke 15:11-32). In another, God was compared to a shepherd who left ninety-nine sheep in the fold, risking his life to search for one who was missing (Luke 15:1-7). In still another, God was like a woman who scoured her house from top to bottom in search of just a single coin and then upon finding it, threw a party to celebrate her good fortune (Luke 15:8-10). Whatever analogy Jesus used, the message was the same: God loves us in a deeply personal way, and God will do the most unexpected things to reach those who are lost and feel cut off from God's love. Jesus taught that if we model our lives after the love of God, a whole new way of living will be opened to us, a life characterized by compassion for all, care for those in need, and forgiveness for those who hurt us.

Of course, sometimes all this talk about love is misunderstood and Jesus is portrayed as a dewy-eyed sentimentalist. Yet, he spoke of a fierce love in ultimate terms. He described it as the kind of love that leads a friend to lay down her or his own life for someone else. To make sure we got the point, he demonstrated this love by his own actions. He once stared down an angry mob preparing to kill a woman who had been caught committing adultery (John 8:1-11), and he even forgave his own executioners when he was being put to death (Luke 23:34). To use a well-worn cliché, Jesus did not just "talk the talk" of love; he walked the way of a love so radical that Christians believe it could have only come from God.

Jesus also revolutionized our understanding of happiness. Some of the best known of Jesus' teachings are found in a series of aphorisms called the Beatitudes. The word *beatitude* means blessedness, and Jesus used this word to describe a deep commitment beyond what we typically call happiness:

Blessed are the poor in spirit,
　　for theirs is the kingdom of heaven.
Blessed are those who mourn,
　　for they will be comforted.
Blessed are the meek,
　　for they will inherit the earth…
Blessed are the peacemakers,
　　for they will be called children of God.

(Matthew 5:3-5, 9)

The following is a contemporary paraphrase of Jesus' prescription for a life well lived:

You're blessed when you're at the end of your rope. With less of you there is more of God and [God's] rule.
You're blessed when you feel you've lost what is most dear to you. Only then can you be embraced by the One most dear to you.
You're blessed when you're content with just who you are—no more, no less. That's the moment you find yourselves proud owners of everything that can't be bought.…
You're blessed when you can show people how to cooperate instead of compete or fight. That's when you discover who you really are, and your place in God's family.

(Matthew 5:3-5, 9; *The Message*)

In contrast to Jesus' teaching are subtle or not-so-subtle cultural messages like these, written by J. B. Phillips, who compares Jesus' beatitudes to contemporary assumptions about happiness:

> You'll be happy when you reach the top of your
>   game.
>   At that pinnacle, you will shine brightly,
>   commanding respect and demanding attention.
> You'll be happy when you've collected the most stuff.
>   Then you will be constantly entertained and the
>   envy of all.
> You'll be happy if you live like a celebrity,
>   consuming, displaying and then discarding
>   everything you can get your hands on.
>   That's the moment when you will feel like a star.
> You'll be happy if you push your way to the top
>   even if it means stepping on a few toes to get
>   there.
>   That's when you will discover how great it is
>   to be number one.

Many of us have tried following such a message, hoping we are on the road to happiness, only to discover that it is a dead-end. Being at the top of our game, collecting the most stuff, and pushing to get ahead do not give meaning to our lives. Jesus offers an alternative. He prescribes a life where happiness is not the goal but a by-product of living in a way that is pleasing to God, a life that makes room for others.

JESUS AS MESSIAH

Jesus began his mission in this way. He traveled to the Jordan River where a man named John was preaching that the Messiah was coming soon. John was called "the Baptist" because he performed the ritual of baptism, using the water of the river to symbolize God's power to cleanse our spirits and help us make a fresh start in life. Jesus came to John and asked to be baptized. John was reluctant because there was something different about Jesus that made the ritual seem unnecessary. But John consented. When Jesus came out of the river, a voice from heaven broke through the clouds and said, "This is my Son, chosen and marked by my love, delight of my life" (Mark 1:11; author's translation).

When the crowd who had gathered around Jesus and John heard God's voice, they knew what this meant. The Savior, whom they called the Messiah or Christ, had finally come. Jewish Scriptures had promised that one day a messenger would be sent from God to re-establish the glory of the Jewish people. An ancient preacher named Isaiah predicted what this divine representative would be like: "Behold, a virgin shall conceive, and bear a son, and shall call his name Immanuel [God-with-Us]....The people that walked in darkness have seen a great light....For unto us a child is born, unto us a son is given: and the government shall be upon his shoulder: and his name shall be called Wonderful, Counsellor, the mighty God, the everlasting Father, the Prince of Peace" (Isaiah 7:14; 9:2, 6 KJV).

In Jesus' day, many of the Jewish people had developed some fairly specific ideas about this one who would rescue them. They expected the Messiah or Christ to be both the representative of God and the avenger of the Jewish people, a powerful warrior and a charismatic political leader (imagine combining General Patton with John F. Kennedy). He would overturn Roman oppression and establish, once and for all, the glory of the nation of Israel. Undoubtedly, the one who was about to appear would be the "Lion of Judah" promised in ancient writings (Jeremiah 49:19).

The day after the baptism when John saw Jesus approaching the river, he shouted, "Here is the Lamb of God!" (John 1:29). "Lamb?" the people must have thought. "What do you mean, lamb? We were expecting a lion." Rather than describing this promised Messiah as a rapacious, terrifying cat on the prowl, John used a term that conjures up something soft and gentle. But the word John used was intentional—and for his audience it would have been familiar. Going back to the earliest days of the Israelite religion, lambs were sacrificed—ritually killed—in worship to make amends to God for a great variety of offenses. Sacrifices were symbolic, a way of expressing the willingness to give up something important in order to say to God, "I'm sorry for the sins I've committed." When John described Jesus as God's lamb, he meant that Jesus was going to rescue them in a way that a military victory never could. Jesus was going to sacrifice himself for us all and somehow make amends for all that had gone wrong in our relationship with God.

In the next chapter, we will consider how this healer, teacher, and Messiah also became our Savior. For now, it is enough to consider that this remarkable person came to be recognized as the Christ, as the Son of God, as God-in-the-flesh. For the very first followers of Jesus, it was obvious that he was human. They traveled with him. They watched him grow tired and hungry. They saw Jesus sleep soundly and eat until he was full. Some watched him die a cruel death at the hand of Roman executioners. At the same time, there was something about Jesus that seemed to go beyond the limits of mere human nature. It was not simply the great miracles he performed, it was also the courageous way he taught people about God with genuine authority. They saw in Jesus a deeper, more personal relationship with God than they had believed possible. Finally, some of those who stayed with him until the end witnessed something remarkable after his execution: they saw him raised from the dead.

After Jesus' resurrection, his followers understood who he was in a whole new way. They began to think of him as being somehow identical with God, without forgetting that he was also human. So, they prayed to him. They worshiped him. They looked to him for help in setting forth on a way that was so radically different from what they were used to, so authentic and so full of joy, that it was as if they had been reborn to a second life.

SHOULD YOU CARE?

Why should you care about Jesus? In so many different ways, people are looking to Jesus Christ to heal them from all that remains broken in their lives, to teach them a new way of responding to the challenges of life, and perhaps even to save them from a path that they have come to view as inauthentic. For two thousand years, people—like the woman at the well—have in a variety of ways seen Jesus in these roles. As you read this, a lonely prisoner may be opening a Bible, reading the story of Jesus in search of hope. A nurse might be doing the same, seeking to model care after the compassion of Jesus. An addict on a street corner and a cancer patient in a hospital may be praying "in the name of Jesus" to hold on and stay strong. The CEO of a large company may be pausing between meetings to pray for a new direction amid the trappings of power and success.

Frederick Buechner once described the hope we all share that one day "life will finally give us the present... which will turn out to be the one that we have waited for so long, which is the one that will fill the empty places. ... But one by one as we open the presents, no matter how rich and wondrous they are, we discover that no one of them by itself, nor even all of them taken together, is the one of our deepest desiring." Some people answer the question "Why should I care about Jesus?" by saying that they have found Jesus Christ to be their healer, their teacher, or even their Messiah. This is a very personal question, and it may be much too early for you to formulate an answer. But we invite you to explore further, to keep your eyes open for something new to happen. If that is where you are, then you will want to keep at least one eye on Jesus Christ and consider who he could be for you.

Three

WHY AM I NOT WHERE I WANT TO BE?

Midway along the journey of life
I woke to find myself in some dark woods,
for I had wandered off from the straight path.
                                    Dante Alighieri

Jesus entered Jericho and was passing through. A man was there by the name of Zacchaeus; he was a chief tax collector and was wealthy. He wanted to see who Jesus was, but being a short man, he could not, because of the crowd. So he ran ahead and climbed a sycamore-fig tree to see him, since Jesus was coming that way.

When Jesus reached the spot, he looked up and said to him, "Zacchaeus, come down immediately. I must stay at your house today." So he came down at once and welcomed him gladly.

All the people saw this and began to mutter, "He has gone to be the guest of a 'sinner.'"

But Zacchaeus stood up and said to the Lord, "Look, Lord! Here and now I give half of my possessions to the poor, and if I have cheated anybody out of anything, I will pay back four times the amount."

Jesus said to him, "Today salvation has come to this house, because this man, too, is a son of Abraham. For the Son of Man came to seek and to save what was lost" (Luke 19:1-10 NIV).

In the days of Jesus, Roman power was at its zenith. Rome both ruled the world and taxed the world. Jericho was a prosperous, beautiful city. Herod the Great, king of the region, had built a beautiful marble palace there for his winter home. Jericho was also the home of a seeker named Zacchaeus. Zacchaeus held the extremely lucrative position of chief tax collector for Rome in the Jericho region. This meant that he was probably not only the richest person in town (at least when King Herod was away) but also the most despised. Actually, despised may be an understatement. One of the Jewish laws of the time reads this way: "If a murderer comes into your house, you are to scrub upon his departure the area in which he stood. If a tax collector comes into your house, you are to scrub the entire house." In those days tax collectors were something like government-sponsored loan sharks, though they did not have to go to the trouble of lending any money. They would simply charge any amount they chose for taxes and keep for themselves everything above the actual tax rate. To add insult to injury (or usury), Zacchaeus was Jewish. He sold out his own people for power, influence, and wealth.

Yet, one day Jesus passed through Jericho, discovered Zacchaeus perched in a sycamore tree, and extended friendship to the most hated guy in town. After this encounter Zacchaeus did not seem like the same person. This man who had devoted his career to greed and intimidation became the first (and probably last) person in history to bring a punitive judgment on himself. That is, he decided to pay back all those he had swindled four times the money he had received. The man who was once capable of such evil now expressed tremendous remorse and generosity.

Zacchaeus is a reflection of us all. In each of us there is so much potential for both good and evil. Of all of God's creation, we human beings are unique. We are the only creatures capable of love and compassion. We are also the only creatures capable of hatred, cruelty, and self-destruction. We have discovered cures to save us from terrible diseases. We have also developed weapons of mass destruction that threaten to annihilate us. We have started wonderful charities like Habitat for Humanity to help people in need. We have also been the source of terrible tragedies like the Holocaust. We can harness energy from oil, the wind, and the sun. Yet, we have also damaged our environment to the point that we all are at risk. We can rescue abandoned children, but we still abuse children in our homes. Getting to the bottom of who we are, and why we make life so tough, is like trying to pull apart the threads of a spider's web. The heights and depths of our own potential make us a mystery even to ourselves.

Other creatures are just not this way. For them, the potential for both good and evil is limited. A dog is simply what a dog is—a bundle of dog instincts, emotions, and habits. A dog eats when hungry, sleeps when tired, and barks when excited. It would be ridiculous to hold a dog responsible for not living up to a true potential as a dog. When a dog eats an unattended steak, what can we say? We can try to train the dog better, but we cannot hold a dog morally accountable. After all, a dog is only a dog.

Sometimes we say similar things about ourselves. When we catch ourselves engaged in some thoughtless action or saying some unkind word, we shrug our shoulders and repeat that time-honored excuse, "Oh well, I'm only human." But when we say that, we are lying to ourselves. Most of us are born with an innate sense that we must strive to reach our highest potential. Part of our emptiness is the feeling that we somehow do not measure up to who we ought to be.

LOSING OUR WAY

"My Lord God, I have no idea where I am going. I do not see the road ahead of me. I cannot know for certain where it will end.... But I believe that the desire to please you does in fact please you."   *Thomas Merton*

The first words of the Bible are these: "In the beginning...God created the heavens and the earth" (Genesis 1:1). According to the Bible, our beginnings are linked to the creation of the world. At the beginning of time, God looked out at the sun and the moon, the mountains and valleys, the oceans and deserts. God looked at the sunrise on a beach; the moonlight on a lake; and the animals in the sea, sky, and land. God looked at everything in creation and said, "This is good!" Yet, creation was not yet complete. There needed to be a crowning act. So God said, "I will make human beings, and I will make people in my own image" (Genesis 1:26; author's translation). We are the very best creation that God could accomplish. Human beings are nothing less than God's own masterpiece. This is the truth about our beginnings. Yet, alongside this knowledge is the recognition that we have somehow strayed from our origins. Christians sum up the various ways that we turn away from God with the word *sin*. It is the biggest stumbling block that prevents us from living the joyous, authentic lives God wants for us.

Sin is difficult to describe because it carries a lot of baggage. When some of us hear the word sin, we get a little nervous. We fidget in our seats, perhaps conjuring up an image of a red-faced, finger-pointing preacher scowling down at his congregation. If this is your image of sin, the word may make you fearful or perhaps angry at Christians for being judgmental. For others of us, sin is an outdated moralism. It reminds us of quaint Victorian times when people were overly concerned with being proper. If this is your notion of sin, the word may bring a smile to your face as you recall the last time someone referred to a dessert as "positively sinful." Our attitudes about sin often slip into simplistic extremes, evoking either the stern Jonathan Edwards, who preached a sermon called "Sinners in the Hands of an Angry God," or actress Mae West (1892–1980), who is said to have quipped, "When choosing between two evils, I always take the one I've never tried before."

In the Bible, sin is rebellion against God, a wrong turn in the direction of our lives. When the great poet Dante portrayed sin, he wrote that he found himself in some dark woods, "for I had wandered off from the straight path." Sin lies at the heart of our discontent and is the cause of our restlessness. As a result, we experience loneliness, regret, shame, and meaninglessness. Most of all, each of us experiences a general anxiety called guilt. Guilt is a vague sense that I personally am not where I ought to be. I know that something in my life needs to be fixed. I need to be made whole, but I do not know where to start to turn my life around. Yet, if I ask, "What are the roadblocks in my life? What is holding me back?" and answer these questions, the answer almost always comes back the same: "What is in my way is me."

We lose our way in a variety of ways. No one plans on taking a wrong turn. As John Ortberg reminds us, "Nobody nurses a grudge in hopes of becoming a bitter, resentful person. People don't give birth to children intending to be so busy that their kids won't know them. No one sits down and plans on having a mediocre existence.... It just happens." One bad choice leads to another until we are too far gone to find our way back.

In his book *Lost in the Cosmos*, Walker Percy conducts experiments designed to reveal what complicated creatures we are. In one experiment, he asked readers to check which of the following statements applied to them:

1. You are extraordinarily generous, ecstatically loving of the right person, supremely knowledgeable about what is wrong with the country, about people, capable of moments of insight unsurpassed by any scientist or artist or writer in the country.
2. You are of all people in the world probably the most selfish, hateful, envious (e.g., you take pleasure in reading death notices in the newspaper and in hearing of an acquaintance's heart attack), the most treacherous, the most frightened, and above all the phoniest.

The odd thing is that Percy found that sixty percent of all respondents chose both. Maybe that is not inappropriate, since we have such tremendous potential for both good and evil, but we do tend to fluctuate between thinking too much of ourselves or not enough.

We can see this mixed vision of ourselves in the following actual personal ads:

> **Strikingly Beautiful**—Ivy League graduate. Playful, passionate, perceptive, elegant, bright, articulate, original in mind, unique in spirit. I possess a rare balance of beauty and depth, sophistication and earthiness, seriousness, and a love of fun. Professionally successful, perfectly capable of being self-sufficient.... Please reply with a substantial letter describing your background and who you are. Photo essential. (Quoted in Cornelius Plantinga.)

> **Loser Seeks Mate:** Lazy, spoiled, insensitive, irresponsible, insecure, desperate SWM. Hate art, travel, reading, and exercise. Like tuna noodle casserole, miniature golf, and tattoos. Love sitting, sleeping, drinking beer, and watching nature films on TV. YOU, a SWF, former cheerleader with amnesia, earn 100K from a trust fund and would enjoy romantic evenings doing my laundry and cleaning my house...great sense of humor. (Quoted in Robert Fulghum.)

It is hard to imagine which potential mate would be worse: a self-centered winner, impressed with her unique combination of beauty and depth, or a self-satisfied loser with a laundry list of unattractive qualities and a basket of dirty clothing. There are times when we become so taken with ourselves that we forget about God and other people. We become the star of the show. All others, including God, are minor characters or even stagehands. And then there are the times when we are too easily satisfied with our perceived limitations. We welcome the role of the stagehand because we are comfortable with low expectations. When we think too much of ourselves or too little, we miss out on the kind of life that God wants for us. We become something different than we were created to be, and we lose our way.

THE WIDENING CIRCLE OF SIN

"What goes around comes around." By this we usually mean that if we commit a thoughtless and mean-spirited act, we will eventually be on the receiving end of something similar. Yet, it is actually more complicated than that. We are bound together with one another in relationships; and what goes around with me typically comes back to you, and vice versa. When I sin, I cause other people to sin too. It is like the ripple effect of a stone thrown into a pond or a computer virus that silently spreads infection from one hard drive to another. Sometimes the effect is obvious. The abused child grows up to abuse her or his own children. But at other times our behavior remains a mystery to us. In one of Carson McCullers's short stories, a teenager named Pete discovers this hidden impulse to pass on misery:

"If a person admires you a lot you despise him and don't care—and it is the person who doesn't notice you that you are apt to admire. This is not easy to realize. Maybelle Watts, this senior at school, acted like she was the Queen of Sheba and even humiliated me. Yet at this same time I would have done anything in the world to get her attentions. All I could think about day and night was Maybelle until I was nearly crazy. When Sucker [Pete's younger brother] was a little kid and on up until the time he was twelve I guess I treated him as bad as Maybelle treated me."

This is the effect of sin. We absorb cruelty and destructiveness from others and then pass it on like a virus. Sin breeds sin. From the moment of our birth, none of us starts clean. The environment we live in, families, communities, and social systems all scar us for life from the instant we take our first breath. Our potential is restricted by the sins of other people, and others are weakened by our moral failures.

Let's explain the pervasive power of sin this way as an adventure in gardening with one of us narrating:

Last summer, I took up gardening. I purchased four tomato plants, two pepper plants, and a cucumber vine. When I returned home from the store with my tiny little starter plants, I noticed that each plant came with its own instructions. For instance, the cucumber plant apparently needed a wide berth. I was instructed to plant it three feet from the nearest other plant. I fudged a little on the directions—actually, more than a little. The entire width of my whole garden was not much more than three feet, just the right size for one cucumber vine. You can guess what happened. With its little tendrils the cucumber reached over the tomato and pepper plants until it was soon one big, sprawling mess. Now if the cucumber vine had done all of this on top of the ground, can you imagine what was happening under the surface? The roots of all these plants must have been tied up in a spider's web of knots, choking the life out of one another.

This is how sin works within our lives. We are tangled up in one another's rebellion against God. Every little resistance to God's plan for my life—every careless action and thoughtless word—tears down people around me. And, because we are also tangled up in the roots of past sins, both individual and social, the consequences are greater than we could ever imagine. Sin is not just a series of bad choices. It is more sinister than that. At times, sin becomes so pervasive that the only roads available to us are the wrong ones. When all of our sins are compounded with one another, a negative force is unleashed in the world that limits everyone's capacity for goodness.

Christians call this mysterious negative force *evil*. Evil is sin on steroids. It is the mysterious, destructive source behind the big ticket items of human destructiveness such as slavery, the Holocaust, or global terrorism. Some Christians attribute this power to a single entity called Satan. Others feel that there can be no individual source of evil, viewing it simply as what happens when the whole human race turns away from God. Yet, Christians agree that evil is a real power, dramatically disrupting the way life was meant to be.

Sin is a way of life that we seem born to repeat. There is more going on than just choosing terrible role models. Sin takes on a life of its own, mutating into a variety of forms that we call evil. Sin is not just breaking the rules of the game; we are all broken, limping along roads that leave us hopelessly lost. The ailment goes deep into our souls, strangling the life out of us and infecting every relationship. The bottom line is that sin and evil constitute a powerful problem. They corrupt our potential, weaken our resolve, and ruin our relationships.

THE WAY BACK

He breaks the power of canceled sin,
he sets the prisoner free;
his blood can make the foulest clean;
his blood availed for me.

Charles Wesley

In the first chapter, we discussed how our spiritual yearning is often accompanied by the vague feeling that the one thing we need most lies beyond our human experience. Nowhere is this more evident than in our awareness of sin. The realization that we and the whole human race are hopelessly lost leads to the recognition that we cannot find our own way home. We need deliverance. We need someone who knows the way to come meet us where we are and set us on the right path again. Only this can rescue us. Christians believe that this is what Jesus Christ does for us. That is why we call him our Savior. We see Jesus reaching out to save the lost in all aspects of his life but especially in his willingness to die on a cross.

Jesus' death took place on a Friday morning. The Roman authorities led Jesus to a hill outside Jerusalem and hanged him on a wooden cross. Dying on a cross was the cruelest form of execution in the ancient world. It was reserved for the worst criminals. Spikes were driven through Jesus' wrists and feet to attach him to the wooden structure, leaving him suspended above the ground like a scarecrow. The whole weight of his body hung on those spikes. Even the slightest movement must have caused excruciating pain. From noon until three that afternoon, an eerie darkness fell across the city of Jerusalem. Gradually, Jesus' breathing became more and more labored (Mark 15:25-39).

In his last hours, Jesus said many strange and wonderful things that Christians continue to cherish and ponder. He prayed, "Father, forgive those people who did this to me. They did not know what they were doing" (Luke 23:34; author's translation). And his last words were these: "Father, I entrust my spirit into your hands" (Luke 23:46; author's translation). With these words,

Jesus "bowed his head" and died (John 19:30). For Christians, the message behind this horrific death is hopeful: Jesus died on the cross for some hidden, higher purpose of God.

THE BRIDGE

"God wears [God's self] out through the infinite thickness of time and space in order to reach the soul. . . . The soul, starting from the opposite end, makes the same journey that God makes towards it. And that is the cross."
Simone Weil

In the previous chapter, we described Jesus as the Messiah, the Promised One from God. In Jesus' day, people expected the Messiah to be a military leader who would deliver them from political bondage. Yet, Jesus was a different kind of Savior. He chose instead to be the "Lamb of God," the one who sacrifices himself for others. The title "Lamb of God" is reminiscent of the sin offerings of the ancient Hebrews, the ritual killings of lambs made in response to human sin. This was not an attempt to appease an angry God. The ancient Hebrews believed that God loves us in spite of our failures. Yet, they were equally convinced that God is holy (meaning pure) and that divine holiness is incompatible with human sin. For this reason, sacrifices were necessary. They purified a sacred space in the world where sinful human beings could encounter their Creator. These dramatic rituals served as a bridge, allowing persons to reconnect with God.

A similar drama occurs in Jesus' death on the cross. Yet, this time, there is an unexpected reversal. Jesus takes the place of the sacrificial lamb. And, because Jesus is God in the flesh, his "good death" reveals something remarkable about God. God is willing to accept the consequences of our sin. God receives the full measure of human rejection and returns love in its place. In the cross, we encounter God as an ocean of love, absorbing human cruelty and destructiveness without being polluted by them.

Even though the pattern of Jesus' death is reminiscent of sacrificial rituals, it goes beyond them in a significant way. The cross does not merely establish a sacred place where we can approach God. Instead, it is the place where God approaches us. Jesus' death is not about sinful people daring to come before God but about the holy God compelled by love to come to us. This reversal changes everything. From it we learn that God loves without counting the cost. Even when our sin separates us from our Creator, God risks everything to overcome the divide. In the cross God creates a bridge, comes to us, and sets us on the right path again. And even as we begin on this new way, God still takes the initiative. For every step we take toward God, God runs to meet us where we are. The cross is God's bridge, reconciling what sin has torn apart, making a way where once there was none.

THE SIGNPOST

We can also understand the cross as a signpost, pointing the way toward a new direction for our lives in response to what God has done for us. If sin is losing our way, we must redirect our path. In the midst of our wandering away from God into the dark woods of sin, God comes to redirect us homeward. In this way, the cross stands in our lives like a signpost at a crossroad, forcing us to decide which way we will go: toward the dark woods away from the light or back toward God and the light.

In the South, you sometimes see handmade signs along country roads with the imperative "Get Right with God." That may be good advice, but it is awfully difficult to know exactly what it means, much less how to do it. Thankfully, God took the initiative. According to the Bible, there is nothing we can do to get right with God; God has made things right between us.

Christians believe this happens through the cross. God allows us to begin our lives anew. We are invited to take up a new way of life full of compassion, hope, and forgiveness, a life as joyous as God intended for us. The Bible does not clearly define what this new life will be like. Instead, it suggests that there is a transformation, a new orientation, a new set of assumptions about what makes life worth living. Christians seek to grab hold of this opportunity God offers us and to do their best to live out its truth.

There is an old folk tale that comes out of Jericho. Many years after Jesus was executed, an old white-haired man could often be seen in a Jericho garden near the Jerusalem road. The townspeople considered him odd because he would always sit under one particular tree. Sometimes he was even seen to reach out a hand and touch the trunk of the tree, almost with reverence. Finally, someone asked him, "Why do you seem to care so much for that old sycamore tree?" The eyes of the old man brightened, and a smile covered his face. He replied, "Because from the branches of the sycamore tree, I first met the Son of God." For Christians, the wooden cross upon which Jesus was crucified is sacred. This "tree" has become the symbol of our common identity. It marks the place where God comes to meet us while we are still hopelessly lost and shows us the way home.

Where have you lost direction? What signpost is guiding you?

Four

WHAT HAPPENS WHEN I DIE?

In the midst of life, we are in death.
Ninth-Century Prayer

Now that same day two of [Jesus' followers] were going to a village called Emmaus, about seven miles from Jerusalem. They were talking with each other about everything that had happened. As they talked and discussed these things with each other, Jesus himself came up and walked along with them; but they were kept from recognizing him.

[Jesus] asked them, "What are you discussing together as you walk along?"

They stood still, their faces downcast. One of them, named Cleopas, asked him, "Are you only a visitor to Jerusalem and do not know the things that have happened there in these days?"

"What things?" he asked.

"About Jesus of Nazareth," they replied. "He was a prophet, powerful in word and deed before God and all the people. The chief priests and our rulers handed him over to be sentenced to death, and they crucified him; but we had hoped that he was the one who was going to redeem Israel. And what is more, it is the third day since all this took place. In addition, some of our women amazed us. They went to the tomb early this morning but didn't find his body. They came and told us that they had seen a vision of angels, who said he was alive. Then some of our companions went to the tomb and found it just as the women had said, but him they did not see."

[Jesus] said to them, "How foolish you are, and how slow of heart to believe all that the prophets have spoken! Did not the Christ have to suffer these things and then enter his glory?" And beginning with Moses and all the Prophets, he explained to them what was said in all the Scriptures concerning himself.

As they approached the village to which they were going, Jesus acted as if he were going farther. But they urged him strongly, "Stay with us, for it is nearly evening; the day is almost over." So he went in to stay with them.

When [Jesus] was at the table with them, he took bread, gave thanks, broke it and began to give it to them. Then their eyes were opened and they recognized him, and he disappeared from their sight. They asked each other, "Were not our hearts burning within us while he talked with us on the road and opened the Scriptures to us?"

They got up and returned at once to Jerusalem. There they found the Eleven [disciples] and those with them, assembled together and saying, "It is true! The Lord has risen and has appeared to Simon." Then the two told what had happened on the way, and how Jesus was recognized by them when he broke the bread. (Luke 24:13-35 NIV)

The reality of death comes as such a shock to us. We can tell a story from one of us. The first person I ever knew who died was a great-grandmother. Because she had suffered from severe dementia, I only knew of her as someone with a wrinkled face and wide eyes that stared silently at me from her bed covers. I still remember the night at the funeral home with all the people filing by to pay their respects. I kept glancing over at the open casket covered with flowers just to see how many times the chill would go up my back. After this macabre game became old, I explored the funeral home with my brother. When we found the kitchen, we dared each other to open the cabinet doors. Before us were six mason jars that must have been filled with vegetable soup, but we had our own morbid speculations. Something that involved human organs was our best guess. I do not recall much else of the evening, but I do remember the peculiar way all the guests stared at me as I ran past them desperately searching for the nearest exit.

Even as adults, we whistle when we walk past graveyards, trying not to think about the inevitable. Sequestering the elderly and the ill in institutions serves not only their need for comfort and care but also our need—for avoidance. We join gyms, take vitamins, drink more water, and eat certain vegetables in an effort to slow down the aging process. We also prefer to call it the "aging process" instead of the equally appropriate "dying process."

Among more creative trends in dealing with death is the "talking tombstone"—a gravesite computer screen that displays video messages from the deceased. Futurists predict the next big way of denying death will be computer-driven holograms that so accurately emulate our traits that our loved ones will be able to have "conversations" with us even after we are gone. The most popular strategy, however, is still denial. We comfort ourselves with the thought that death is a misfortune that happens to other people. Author Bert States summed up this strategy well when he said, "We wrap death in the social shroud of 'they,' the 'others,' and 'all of us,' as if by generalizing we might third person Death to death."

In spite of our attempts to avoid death, the mortality rate, as Roman Catholic priest Richard John Neuhaus reminds us, "holds steady at 100 percent." To paraphrase the popular bumper sticker, we might say that "Death Happens." And, it happens everywhere we look.

The Bible does not attempt to spare us from this fact of life. An ancient preacher summed up human existence with these words: "For everything there is a season...a time to be born, and a time to die" (Ecclesiastes 3:1-2). Accepting our own death as an inevitable part of life has a way of reordering our priorities. Things like wealth, health, comfort, and popularity are still nice and certainly add value to life, but they no longer seem worthy of our ultimate concern. Other things, such as our relationships with family, friends, and God, take on a new importance in our lives.

CRAVING THE ETERNAL

Learning to face the inevitability of death is, according to Christianity, only part of the answer. It is not just that we are running from that uninvited guest that eventually snares us all. It is also that we are longing for something in our lives that is not subject to loss. Writer Kathleen Norris recalls her visit to a second-grade classroom in South Dakota. As the students struggled to complete their writing assignment, she peered over the shoulder of one little girl who was "sitting halfway in, halfway out of her desk, [with] one leg swinging in the air." This is what the child was busy writing: "When my third snail died, I said, I'm through with snails." This little girl was learning one of life's most difficult lessons: Everything we love comes with an expiration date. So we mourn not just our eventual end but all the cherished objects of childhood we casually toss aside, every old friend we lose touch with, each hometown that is no longer what it used to be, the sad realization that life itself is fleeting.

A man once told about his relationship with his wife, describing the good times they shared as well as the difficult last two years of her life when as an invalid she deteriorated rapidly—physically and mentally. He concluded with a short discourse on the unfairness of death: "She lived to be seventy-five. I guess I should be grateful for that. Some would say that this is a ripe old age, that she had a full life. You want to know what I say? I say it was not long enough!" There is something in all of us that protests death, that says this life and its allotment of days is not enough. For this man death came like an intruder, robbing him of a deep, abiding companionship that gave his life meaning, of a person who needed him and inspired him with a sense of purpose.

One of the most troubling things about death is that it seems to rob our activities of their meaning. Sometimes we say, "No one will care in one hundred years." While this is meant to put our ambitions and desires in perspective, it also robs them of their meaning. All of us want the kind of life in the present that will still reverberate with meaning thousands of years from now. We want lasting significance. This yearning helps us understand that what we desire is not just an extension of the present. We do not want our days to drag on through eternity just as they are now. We long for a different kind of life, a fuller life that is imbued with meaning and purpose.

Thornton Wilder vividly portrays this authentic life in his play *Our Town*. Emily, a young woman who dies in childbirth, is allowed by the godlike Stage Manager to go back and observe a single day in her brief life. The dead advise her to "choose the least important day in your life. It will be important enough." Emily selects her twelfth birthday and is overwhelmed by her experience of ordinary things like sunflowers and coffee, "new-ironed dresses and hot baths...and sleeping and waking up...I didn't realize. So all that was going on and we never noticed." She looks toward the Stage Manager and asks abruptly, through her tears, "Do any human beings ever realize life while they live it?—every, every minute?" The Stage Manager answers, "No...The saints and poets, maybe—they do some."

What would such a deep, authentic life look like? For many, it would be characterized by love. This craving for lasting love can be heard in pop songs that serenade the "real thing," the one love that will save us, will make our life worthwhile. Yet, even in our most treasured experiences of love, we often feel like something is still missing, that there is something more. What we crave is a different kind of love—a love that unconditionally accepts us as we are and values us without measure. In short, we want the kind of love that can only come from God. This kind of love gives our lives true and lasting meaning. This kind of love is so enduring that it would require a life without end to experience it fully.

THE RESURRECTION

"The resurrection transcends this life—it was no magic resuscitation reversing the actuality of a cruel death, but an anticipation of a totally new order of existence, God's new creation."   Frances Young

Christians place their hope for life beyond death in the resurrection of Jesus Christ. As Jesus hung on the cross, he cried out in a loud voice, "It is finished" (John 19:30).

What was finished? His life. Jesus "gave up his spirit," and he died (John 19:30). This is remarkable if you believe Jesus to be God in the flesh. Even God knows what it is like to lose everything—even life itself. Yet, this time something was different. God was not defeated by death. While in every other biography death is the final chapter, Jesus' death was the beginning of something more.

When Jesus' body was taken off the cross on a Friday afternoon, most of his followers were nowhere to be found. His disciples were in hiding. Yet, two of Jesus' followers, a man named Joseph and Nicodemus (the inquirer who had come to Jesus in the middle of the night; see Chapter 1 of this book) stayed to the bitter end. They respectfully wrapped Jesus' body in a white cloth and placed it in a tomb cut out of solid rock in the side of a hill. When the men had laid Jesus' body in the tomb, they rolled a large stone against its entrance (John 19:38-42).

According to the Gospel of Matthew, on the Sunday morning after Jesus' death, two other close friends of Jesus, "Mary Magdalene and the other Mary," came to the stone tomb (Matthew 28:1). The women encountered something totally unexpected. An angel descended from heaven, rolled the stone away, and spoke: "There is nothing to fear here. I know you're looking for Jesus, the One they nailed to the cross. Jesus is not here. He was raised from the dead" (Matthew 28:5-6; author's translation). Filled with a combination of shock and joy, they rushed back to where the disciples were hiding and told them what had happened.

Over the next forty days, Jesus appeared to many of his followers (Luke 24:13-53; Acts 1:1-5). His resurrection is a sign of hope unprecedented in human history. If death is our ultimate enemy, then, at least in this instance, it has finally been conquered.

IS THE RESURRECTION TRUE?

The challenge of believing in the Resurrection is described in the biblical story of Thomas, one of Jesus' followers. Upon news that others had seen Jesus after his death, Thomas exclaimed that he would only believe the Resurrection actually happened if he saw the holes in Jesus' hands made by the spikes that nailed him to the cross. One day Jesus appeared to Thomas. He gently took Thomas's hand and instructed him, "Put your finger here and see my hands." Thomas was neither scolded nor ridiculed for his reservations. On the contrary, Jesus seems to have understood Thomas's doubt (John 20:24-29).

Such doubt is natural. Many people still wonder if the Resurrection actually occurred. Alternative possibilities have been proposed. Some skeptics say that Jesus' body must have been stolen from the tomb before anyone arrived. Other critics have suggested that since Jesus' followers were overwhelmed with grief, his appearances to them after his death could be explained as collective hallucinations.

Yet, it does seem clear that something truly remarkable had taken place. A group of defeated and despondent men and women suddenly became brave witnesses. They were willing to be tortured and killed rather than forsake their experience of the Resurrection. This is quite a transformation for a group of people who were in hiding while Jesus was being executed. They were willing to die themselves because they had come to believe that death no longer has the final word.

WHAT DIFFERENCE DOES IT MAKE?

"In all the tragic dramas of antiquity . . . the hero . . . reaches his pinnacle only to be cut down. Only in the drama of Jesus does the opposite pattern hold: the hero is cut down only to be raised up." Thomas Cahill

If you have attended an Easter worship service—when Christians celebrate the resurrection of Jesus—you may remember being stirred by trumpets accompanying the choir, enjoying the beauty of lilies in the sanctuary, and feeling a special excitement in the air. The psychologist Rollo May once wrote about attending an Easter celebration in Greece. The church was dark, lit only by candles; and the service was in a language that was difficult for him to understand. But at the climax of the service, the priest presented three beautifully decorated Easter eggs and announced, "Christo Anesti!"—"Christ is Risen!" Later, May reflected on what that experience meant to him. He wrote, "I was seized then by a moment of spiritual reality: What would it mean for our world if He had truly risen?" This is a good question, and Christians believe that it is answered in two ways: by the living presence of Jesus Christ in our lives and by the promise that we, too, will experience new life after death.

The risen Jesus appeared to the disciples over a period of forty days. One of the last things he told them before ascending into heaven was this: "I am with you always, to the end of the age" (Matthew 28:20). Christians believe that Jesus Christ does continue with us. The miracle that occurred on the first Easter was not just the resuscitation of a corpse. Jesus was not raised only to die again at a later time. Easter was something brand new. It was a resurrection. Christians believe he will never die and that God is present to us today through the risen Jesus Christ.

This has the potential to alter our approach to life radically. The night before Jesus was killed, he anticipated the terrible loss his disciples were about to suffer and prepared them with a promise that impacts us all. He assured them that he would not leave them desolate but would send a Comforter, called the Holy Spirit, to be with them (and with us). The Holy Spirit is another way of saying that God is intimately present to us through the risen Christ. Even though Jesus lived two thousand years before us, his Spirit walks alongside us—providing comfort when we are heartbroken, guidance when we feel lost, and joy as we are led into deeper relationship with God. Through the Holy Spirit, God remains vitally and intimately connected with us—more supportive than even our closest friends. We have the assurance that we are not alone in the universe. God is with us, vitally present, through Jesus Christ.

Author Philip Yancey sums up the difference this makes: "In the Spirit, God has found a way to live within me, helping me from the inside out. God has not promised a state of constant bliss or a problem-free existence but has promised to be present in the silence and in the dark, to exist alongside us, within us and for us."

The Resurrection also holds out the hope that for us death is not the end. We believe that Jesus conquered death and that through him we can share in the promise of new life. Before he died, Jesus promised us that we would somehow participate in this miracle, that he had conquered death for us all. He once told his disciples, "In my Father's house are many rooms; if it were not so, I would have told you. I am going there to prepare a place for you" (John 14:2 NIV). This too makes a profound difference in the way we live. Rather than avoiding death, rather than going through life pretending that death is something that happens to everybody but us, we can confront this reality and accept death for what it is: a threshold to something brand new. Christians see death not as a period but as a comma. Like the first witnesses, we believe that death is not the final chapter in the story of our lives but an introduction to an entirely new narrative. The Resurrection also completely changes how we experience the death of people we love. We believe that everyone who follows Jesus Christ will die, but his followers will also live beyond death.

The quality of our living is determined in large measure by the attitude we take toward our dying. The Resurrection unlocks the secret to a purposeful, authentic life in which we are afraid of nothing. We discover that the meaning of life comes from giving up our lives for others and believing that not even death will separate us from God's love.

WHAT HAPPENS WHEN WE DIE?

"I think that the dying pray at the last not 'please' but 'thank you' as a guest thanks his host at the door. Falling from airplanes the people are crying thank you, thank you, all down the air."   *Annie Dillard*

Throughout human history, people have asked, "Is there life after death?" The question has been answered in many different ways. Some people say that nothing happens when we die, that death is the end of existence, that we are snuffed out like a candle, that people remain alive only in the memories of those who are left behind. Other people see death as a passage to another, different kind of earthly existence. This concept of reincarnation views life as a "wheel of existence" where each person's essential self is endlessly transmuted into another being from one generation to the next. Finally, many people believe in the immortality of the soul. It is often confused with the Christian view of life after death. Ancient Greeks believed that there is a portion of each of us, called the soul, that is unique to each person, indivisible, indestructible, and eternal. During earthly existence the soul is imprisoned in a mortal body. At death, the physical body dies and decays; but the soul lives on, freed from limitations.

Christians believe that each of us is a unique combination of body and soul. We are singular individuals who have been given the breath of God. In death, the body and soul expire. Yet, death is not the end. In life after death, both soul and body are resurrected. God responds to the yearning for lasting meaning, enduring love, and ongoing life with the promise of a new life that transcends death and that is lived in closer communion with our Creator. We believe that there is some essential continuity between who we are today and who we will become after we die. We do not know exactly what this new body after death will be like, but we do know that we will be renewed in some form. The persons we are now, in our fullest sense, will be resurrected to a new life with God. This is the hope that we receive from Jesus' resurrection. This is the victory that God has won for us against our common enemy, death.

The Christian notion of life after death does not just refer to the continuation of the soul as a kind of survival capsule that outlasts the body. And death is more than just a flimsy door through which the soul escapes from the body. Death is final, but through death God recreates everything that makes us unique. God does not just revive us but renews us as complete persons.

WHAT ABOUT HEAVEN AND HELL?

"Joy is the serious business of heaven."　　　*C. S. Lewis*

"Sin is man's way of telling God to leave him alone. Hell is God's way of saying okay."　　　*Modern Proverb*

The Bible uses metaphors to help us picture what the next life may be like. Heaven is described in pastoral terms as a beautiful garden, an orchard, or a charming wooded area. It is also described in urban terms as a vibrant, bustling city full of free, dynamic citizens. Perhaps the variety of images means that we should not be so concerned with exactly what heaven will be like. It may be that there is something different for everyone in heaven—a place with at least as much variety as our earthly world. Still, one cannot help but wonder if the things we enjoy here will be available to us in heaven. Anglican Archbishop Desmond Tutu once said, "I wonder whether they have rum and Coke in heaven? Maybe it's too mundane a pleasure, but I hope so—as a sundowner. Except, of course, the sun never goes down there. Oh, man, this heaven is going to take some getting used to."

One consistent theme is that heaven is where we are free from the things that hold us back in this world. We are free from sabotaging our relationship with God through sin. We are free from the violence in the world and the malice that ruins relationships. We are free to love others and to love ourselves, free from the ceaseless competition and self-loathing that characterizes so much of our present lives. Christians contend that human beings are most real in heaven because there they are simply themselves. Our resurrected life will not be in any way less than our present existence. In the richness of our relationships, in the depth of our intimacy with God, it will in fact be more.

When you were a young child, you may have thought of living in heaven as being assigned to your own cloud, wearing a white robe, and spending the better part of your days plucking harp strings. We assume that heaven will be nothing like our lives on earth. The Christian faith does not present heaven as something that is totally different from life on earth, however. It is instead a wonderful extension of all that is good and true right here. It is not just an extension of time but a new depth of experience. For example, most of us love summer produce. Every spring we begin looking forward to homegrown tomatoes, fresh peaches, and watermelons. Yet, after a winter of eating canned fruits and shipped vegetables, we can barely remember what they taste like. That first July peach or August tomato makes us think, *So this is what peaches and tomatoes are supposed to taste like.* Perhaps heaven is something like this experience. It is not the opposite of life on earth but a deeper, more intense experience of all that we already love about our lives. Its pleasures are not less real but instead are more real than we can imagine. In heaven we discover a new kind of relationship with God, free from all that we have lost through sin. It is the place where we reach new levels of fulfillment, becoming more and more like Jesus while remaining essentially ourselves.

While heaven is a harmonious place of closer communion with God, hell has been depicted as a place of chaos, of complete separation from God. Christians are divided as to whether hell is a place of punishment or a state of nonbeing where those who refuse the joys of God's presence are allowed to slip away from life. More important than where exactly hell is or what it looks like is the possibility that in the life beyond, we may have no relationship with God. Like heaven, hell, too, may be more a state of being than an actual place. It may be the condition in which the refusal to relate to God gradually numbs one from the joys of the new until one gradually withers away. Hell, it seems, is reserved for people not because they have performed some specific evil actions, but because they have chosen not to be in a relationship with God. Hell may be but a self-imposed prison. The novelist Dorothy Sayers puts it this way: "There is no power in this world or the next that can keep a soul from God if God is what it really desires. But, if in seeing God, the soul rejects [God] in hatred and horror, then there is nothing more that God can do for it…but give it what it desires."

We began this chapter with a story from the Bible about two followers of Jesus: a man named Cleopas and an unnamed companion. Because women were often not mentioned by name in ancient texts, it has often been suggested that these two heartbroken disciples may have been a married couple. We can imagine that this couple barely speak to each other. Their downcast eyes rarely leave the road before them. It was only a week ago that they came to Jerusalem to be with Jesus. Now they are leaving that city. Jesus is dead, and the only thing left to do is to return home and put their foolish dreams behind them. Death, we have always assumed, is where all our dreams end.

Yet, what if the Resurrection actually happened? How would your life be changed? For one thing, Jesus would no longer be just a miraculous healer and great teacher of the past, he could also be your Savior, reconciling you to God not merely once upon a time, but here in your life today. You could also live with hope that sustains you in life and death, with hope that with Jesus Christ there is still more to come. As with this couple on the road to Emmaus, grief and loss would remain; but they would be put in a new context. For like this couple, you might experience the presence of a mysterious companion on the road. You might find that even though you have not always recognized him, Jesus Christ has been with you all along the journey.

Five

CAN I TRUST GOD?

God is frightful. God is great—you pick. I choose this.
God is in the details, the completely unnecessary miracles
sometimes tossed up as stars to guide us. . . . Look hard
enough and you'll see them.   *Barbara Kingsolver*

Moses was keeping the flock of his father-in-law Jethro, the priest of Midian; [Moses] led his flock beyond the wilderness, and came to Horeb, the mountain of God. There the angel of the LORD appeared to him in a flame of fire out of a bush; he looked, and the bush was blazing, yet it was not consumed. Then Moses said, "I must turn aside and look at this great sight, and see why the bush is not burned up." When the LORD saw that he had turned aside to see, God called to him out of the bush, "Moses, Moses!" And, he said, "Here I am." Then [God] said, "Come no closer! Remove the sandals from your feet, for the place on which you are standing is holy ground." [God] said further, "I am the God of your father, the God of Abraham, the God of Isaac, and the God of Jacob." And Moses hid his face, for he was afraid to look at God.

Then the LORD said, "I have observed the misery of my people who are in Egypt; I have heard their cry on account of their taskmasters. Indeed, I know their sufferings, and I have come down to deliver them from the Egyptians, and to bring them up out of that land to a good and broad land, a land flowing with milk and honey....So come, I will send you to Pharaoh to bring my people, the Israelites, out of Egypt." But Moses said to God, "Who am I that I should go to Pharaoh, and bring the Israelites out of Egypt?" [God] said, "I will be with you; and this shall be the sign for you that it is I who sent you: when you have brought the people out of Egypt, you shall worship God on this mountain."

But Moses said to God, "If I come to the Israelites and say to them, 'The God of your ancestors has sent me to you,' and they ask me, 'What is his name?' what shall I say to them?" God said to Moses, "I AM WHO I AM." [God] said further, "Thus you shall say to the Israelites, 'I AM has sent me to you.'"..."Thus you shall say to the Israelites, 'The LORD, the God of your ancestors, the God of Abraham, the God of Isaac, and the God of Jacob, has sent me to you':

> This is my name forever,
> and this my title for all
> generations." (Exodus 3:1-15)

Perhaps it was one of those perfect fall evenings, clear and crisp with a bright harvest moon in the sky. Having finished your dinner, you decided to take a walk. For some reason, in the middle of your walk, you stopped. You looked up at the stars, breathed in the fall air, and for that one moment everything in the universe just seemed to come together. An unexpected assurance washed over you as you thought, *All of this couldn't have been an accident.* Or maybe it was a summer beach trip with your family, the time you woke up before anyone else to see the sunrise. As that orange glow hit the water for the first time, you just knew that we are not alone; someone must have orchestrated the wonders of creation. Each of us has probably experienced an unexpected certainty that a wise Creator must be out there somewhere.

Yet, as powerful as such a feeling can be, it does not answer the most important question. Even if we feel certain there is a God, we still do not know what kind of God is "out there." So, as we go about our lives, we imagine God in all sorts of ways: a spectator who silently watches us from a distance, an aloof judge in a black robe, a grizzled grandfather with a long white beard. Most of us never completely outgrow the speculations of our childhood. Anne Lamott observes that for many of us, God remains "a high school principal in a gray suit who never remembered your name but is always leafing unhappily through your files." Or we may just throw up our hands and agree with Lisa from the animated television series *The Simpsons*, who says to her brother, Bart, "I don't know who or what God is exactly. All I know is he's a force more powerful than Mom and Dad put together."

Of course there are times when we long to know more than this. A friend dies. A relationship ends. A new job does not work out. A nation confronts terrorism. When tragedy strikes, we need a more grown-up conception of God. No longer satisfied with the vague sense that God must be "out there," we begin to ask more probing questions: "Does God really care what happens to me?" "Will God still be there when things get tough?" "Can I trust God to be my guide?"

Moses also wondered about these things. (You may remember him from the DreamWorks film *The Prince of Egypt*.) Moses was the great leader of the Hebrew people, the one who dared to challenge Egypt's pharaoh and demand that the Hebrews be liberated after hundreds of years of slavery. Moses was the one who bravely marched the terrified former slaves across the parted waters of the Red Sea to the first real freedom they had ever known. But before any of this happened, Moses was a lot like us. He was an inquirer, longing to know who God really is and searching for a sense of purpose in his life.

When Moses stumbled upon that mysterious bush on Mount Horeb, he was living as an outlaw. Back in Egypt he had a price on his head. In a fit of rage, he had killed an Egyptian who was brutally beating a Hebrew slave. With that one act Moses had blown his bright future in Egypt's government. He must have wondered if he could trust God to guide him through this mess, if God really cared about him at all. In the midst of this desperate searching, God came and found him, offering a message that would change his life and alter the history of the Hebrew people. What Moses heard that day must have come as a greater shock than the fiery bush that somehow remained as green as if it had just been watered. God said, "I have observed the misery of my people. . . . I have heard their cry. . . . I know their sufferings. . . . I will send you to Pharaoh to bring my people...out of Egypt" (Exodus 3:7-10).

Understandably skeptical about this ancient version of *Mission Impossible*, Moses asked God whom he should say had sent him. The voice rang out with a cryptic response: "I AM WHO I AM" (Exodus 3:14). No one knows for sure what God meant by this, but it seems that God was reminding Moses that God, the Creator of the universe, can be anything God chooses. This sounds awfully intimidating. In the original biblical language, however, this sentence suggests that God "is" or "exists" and "causes to be" in the present and in the future. God sees our suffering. God knows when we are hurting, and God has chosen to be the one who will help us through to the other side. And, according to the Bible, that is exactly what God did.

Not only was this good news for Moses, it is good news for the rest of us too. First, it changes everything about our search for God. We realize that we are seeking the very One who inspired our search in the first place. We are longing to find the One who has already found us. We yearn to know the One who desires nothing more than to be known by us. Next, it has the potential to change our whole approach to life. If God has already decided to stand beside us no matter what, then we do not have to feel so alone anymore. What is more, those terrible tragedies of life—the personal failures, the heartbreak, the seemingly hopeless situations—that stand in our way may not be impassible after all. God is in the business of liberation. God yearns to free us from all those things that pin us down and keep us from reaching our true potential. Our God is the God who makes a way when there is no way.

GOD'S PLAN

Sometimes we feel as if we are at the mercy of random events—from car wrecks to corporate downsizing, from unwanted pregnancies to acts of terrorism. Yet, Christians refuse to believe that history is merely random. Beneath the apparent disorder of our lives and the chaos of world events, God has a plan that endows human history with meaning and purpose. We see this in two names that Christians use for God. We call God both "Creator" and "Sustainer." God brings the universe into existence and sets the course of human history. Yet, God also preserves the world, ensuring that one day history will reach its proper conclusion. Of course, God does this in subtle, unexpected ways. God is more like an artist painting in broad strokes than an iron-fisted dictator who manipulates by divine decree. God chooses to woo us rather than to rule over us. God picks intimacy over intervention.

This is who God has been all along. God's intentions are clear from the start. Above all else, God desires a special relationship with every woman, man, and child. Genesis says that human beings were created in the image of God (1:27) and that God walked with them in the cool evening breezes (3:8-9). Even when the man and woman disobeyed God and suffered the consequences, God "made garments of skins…and clothed them" (3:21).

A covenant is a formal agreement between two people, but it is much closer to a marriage vow than to a business contract. It is a solemn promise always to be there for the other person in every possible way. God promised Noah to protect the earth (Genesis 9:8-11). God promised Abraham and Sarah that they would become parents of a great nation (Genesis 17). God promised Moses and the people of Israel that "I am" would always be with them, no matter what (Exodus 3:12). Because God's promises, unlike human ones, are not made to be broken, the covenant God makes is unwavering. God is steadfast, staying in relationship with us whether we are aware of it or not, whether we greet it joyfully or try to evade it, whether we express this truth in the way we live or do everything we can to deny it. We cannot weaken God's commitment. What God decides is set in stone; and before God determined anything else about our world, God decided to love us.

God's plan is that we will reciprocate this love, living out our days in intimacy with our Creator and extending this harmony to other people and to the world around us. But God does not force us to make this choice. One of the peculiar things about covenants is that they require freedom from both parties. Just as a "shotgun wedding" is no true marriage at all, our participation in God's covenant cannot be compulsory. God hopes that we will freely choose this. Freedom is a double-edged sword, however; and in order to be free to accept it, we must also be free to reject it. Out of deep respect for us, God allows us to be free—free to stay or free to walk away.

HUMAN SUFFERING

From our earlier discussions, you probably already know that we often choose to walk away. The *modus operandi* of the human race is to reject what God offers. We all do this to some degree or another. As countless generations have gone against the grain of God's plan, the result is a world of hurt. According to Christianity, suffering is not a sign that God is uncaring or punitive. Suffering runs the gamut. It includes personal heart-break; family tragedies; national crises; and even earth pains, which the Bible poetically describes as creation "groaning" (Romans 8:22). It emerges from illness, nat-ural disasters, and other sources beyond human control. Poignant suffering may well result from a choice to act with mercy or justice in spite of cultural disapproval. Fre-quently, however, our suffering results from tragic human choices.

Often the greatest hurt in our lives comes not from what others do to us, but from what we do to ourselves. Human sin typically leads to suffering not because God is punishing us but because we have lost our way. God created us to share a unique relationship with our Creator and then to extend the love we experience with God to other people and to the world around us. But we have cut ourselves off from our life source. We are disconnected from the persons we were meant to become, and this weakens our relationships to other people and to the world.

For instance, part of God's covenant with us included the gift of creation. We were given the world in which we live as a sacred trust, and we were commissioned to be the earth's caretakers. Yet, look at what we have done with this gift: We have polluted its waters and ruined its soil; we have irrevocably damaged the very air that we breathe. When dangerous new diseases spring up or we face the terrible consequences of global warming, we cannot claim that God is untrustworthy.

In India, there is a story of a highly respected elder who was confronted by youngsters plotting to embarrass him. One youngster held a beautiful bird behind his back. The group said to the elder, "There's a bird; is it alive or dead?" If he replied, "It is alive," the youngster would kill the bird by squeezing its neck to prove the elder was wrong. If he replied, "It is dead," the youngster would release the bird to fly away and again prove the elder wrong. When the youngsters repeated three times, "There's a bird; is it alive or dead?" the elder thought deeply and replied, "It is in your hands."

It is the same with us. Covenants by nature make demands. We are free to accept or reject them. If we choose the latter, there will be negative consequences, not because God is punishing us, but because that is the nature of true freedom. God made us to be the caretakers of creation, but the choice is ours. The world is in our hands.

GOD'S RESPONSE

Jesus teaches us that God is our Father. Jesus called God "Abba," an informal word in the ancient Aramaic language for Father, something akin to "Papa" or "Daddy" (Mark 14:36). The last words that Jesus uttered before his death were, "Father, into your hands I commend my Spirit" (Luke 23:46). Jesus understood God in a deeply personal, intimate way, so much so that Christians primarily view God as the "Father of our Lord Jesus Christ" (Romans 15:6). God is not only the Father of Jesus, God is the Father of us all. Jesus summed up the way God feels about us with a single, poignant reminder. If you and I know how to give good things to our children, how much more will our heavenly Father give good things to us—the children of God (Matthew 7:7-11).

When Jesus called God "Father," he was not trying to say anything about God's gender. He was not suggesting that God is some magnified image of our earthly fathers. If you have had a difficult father, the idea that God is a divine version of an earthly father may be deeply disturbing. Jesus was not saying that God is a potentially aggressive or inattentive male.

What is important is not the word we use for God but the message that Jesus was trying to get across. We learn from Jesus that God's love for us can be compared to the highest expressions of human affection, to the feelings of a strong mother or a compassionate father. He wanted us to know that God is like our image of an ideal parent—a parent who is infinitely kind, patient, and loving. He wanted us to be assured that God is deeply concerned about us, vitally interested in our well-being.

When we make things go wrong, God responds with passion. Like any good parent, God shares in our pain and suffering. Any mother or father knows that as parents we are not only aware of the sufferings of our children, we actually participate when our children hurt. We find ourselves lying awake at night worrying about their well-being. Our children's welfare becomes more important than anything else. It is that way for God. In one of the oldest books of the Bible, God's relationship to Israel (called by the ancient name "Ephraim") is portrayed like that of a heartbroken parent experiencing the pain of rejection:

> When Israel was a child, I loved him,
>   and out of Egypt I called my son.
> The more I called them,
>   the more they went from me;
> they kept sacrificing to Baals [popular ancient gods],
>   and offering incense to idols.
>
> Yet it was I who taught Ephraim to walk,
>   I took them up in my arms;
>   but they did not know that I healed them.
> I led them with cords of human kindness,
>   with bands of love.
> I was to them like those
>   who lift infants to their cheeks.
>   (Hosea 11:1-4)

When we want to express to small children that we think they are special, we might say, "You're the apple of my eye." This phrase actually comes from the Bible. An ancient poet in an Old Testament book of songs once asked that God watch over him as if he were the apple of God's eye (Psalm 17:8). This ancient phrase could be translated as "the little man of the eye." It points to the experience of looking directly into someone's eye so closely that you see an image of yourself in the eye of the other person. Think of two teenagers at a pizza parlor who stare so intently at each other that they seem to be trying to hypnotize each other. An even better example might be a mother breastfeeding her child. Psychologists tell us that during those long extended gazes when she looks directly into her infant's eyes, she experiences many of the same emotions as a lovesick teenage couple. Quite literally, she falls in love with her baby, and the baby falls in love with her. This is what it means to be the apple of someone's eye. According to the Bible, this is how God looks at each of us. Each one of us is the apple of our Creator's eye.

In her book *Amazing Grace*, Kathleen Norris tells about watching a young couple with an infant at an airport departure gate: "The baby was staring intently at other people, and as soon as he recognized a human face, no matter whose it was, no matter if it was young or old, pretty or ugly, bored or happy or worried-looking he would respond with absolute delight. It was beautiful to see....I felt...awe-struck...because I realized that this is how God looks at us, staring into our faces in order to be delighted, to see the creature he made and called good, along with the rest of creation."

That is the way love is. When you are in love with someone, you see all the little things about her or him that others do not bother to notice. We see this expressed by a wide variety of writers of love songs from Cole

Porter to Coldplay. God notices all the little things about us. God longs to know each of us more deeply and in even greater detail than our best friends, our spouses, or our parents. The Bible puts this in the strongest terms possible. Jesus said that God has the number of hairs on our head numbered (Matthew 10:30); and an ancient poet expressed God's concern with this beautiful prayer:

> For it was you who formed my inward parts;
>   you knit me together in my mother's womb...
> Wonderful are your works...
> My frame was not hidden from you,
> when I was being made in secret...
> Your eyes beheld my unformed substance.
>
> (Psalm 139:13-16)

Christians believe that since God remains present to us in the midst of suffering, our most difficult times may become an opportunity for growth. In a way, life is structured like this. Every advance we make comes through pain. Infants learn to sleep through the night only through the anxiety of being separated from their parents. Toddlers learn to walk only by falling down a lot. Adolescents learn about love through bouts of insecurity and disappointment. Older adults gain wisdom as they live with the loss of friends and family. Suffering is a part of life, and God speaks to us through suffering. God speaks through illness, injustice, and misunderstandings to bring us to a singleminded attention to that which will bring us an authentic life. God works through suffering to lead us to make important decisions in our lives. Suffering may be painful, but it is also an opportunity. It may lead us to focus on the essentials and to leave the rest behind.

Wouldn't it be easier to abolish suffering altogether or at least write "I Love You" in the sky? We tend to imagine God intervening from above. But it may be that God chooses to help us grow through the suffering of life. God makes provisions for us beneath the surface of things. God chooses not to abolish suffering, but to help us grow through the pain of life, to grow and find meaning within the suffering of life.

Western culture often views occasions of suffering as meaningless tragedies. The Christian vision is that suffering has meaning. Jesus is said to have taken on himself both our suffering and the sinful choices that often cause suffering. In God's hands suffering has a beneficial power that transforms it into something that at least potentially has power to produce positive results in our lives.

William Sloane Coffin was a well-known Presbyterian minister a generation ago. One night his twenty-four-year-old son, Alex, was killed when his car crashed through a guard rail and into Boston Harbor. A few days after his death, Coffin was asked if his son's death was the will of God. He replied, "God doesn't go around the world with his fingers on triggers, his fist around knives, his hands on steering wheels....My own consolation lies in knowing that it was not the will of God that Alex die; that when the waves closed over the sinking car, God's heart was the first to break." But it was not merely the thought of a heartbroken God that brought Coffin comfort. He also believed that God's plans for Alex were not foiled even by death. The accident had been terrible. Alex would never grow up to be the gentle, thoughtful man he seemed destined to become. Yet, even in death, Alex was not cut off from the love of God. Coffin expressed his hope in Alex's new life with God in poetic terms: "If a week ago last Monday a lamp went out, it was because for [Alex] at least, the Dawn had come."

This does not mean that God had some hidden purpose in mind when Alex was killed. On the contrary, his death went against the grain of God's will. Rather than working out some higher plan by causing us to suffer, God chooses to suffer with us. Because God makes this choice, suffering may be painful, discouraging, even humiliating at times, but it is never meaningless. God works within such situations to help us find meaning and purpose. For Alex, God offered the promise of a new life in Christ after his death. For Alex's father, God provided hard-earned wisdom that would allow him to help others in the midst of tragedy. Such blessings never make up for tragic loss, but they do make it possible for those who are left behind to continue living with dignity and meaning. These blessings give us the hope that even those who are taken from us are not at an end. They have the promise of a new life. God makes a way when there is no way.

God loves us so much that God chooses to experience what we experience. So at one point in history, God actually became one of us (John 1). In Jesus, God comes all the way to where we are, willing to experience pain, loneliness, and all the limitations that come with being human. Earlier, we said that one of the ways Jesus saves us is by establishing a new solidarity with God. Now we can put it in even stronger terms. Because God suffers with us in Jesus, there is an intimacy between God and us that we would never have imagined on our own. Through Jesus, God experienced suffering in many different ways. After a long journey, he knew fatigue. When a friend died, he wept with grief. When his followers deserted him, he knew the pain of betrayal. Before his execution, he was whipped, beaten, and kicked. On the cross, nails were driven into his wrists. He cried out in despair to God, and his life slipped away.

This act of solidarity, above all others, erased all the difference between God and us. In Jesus, God experienced the worst of what life on earth had to offer. Episcopal priest Barbara Brown Taylor imagines God addressing all of us with the impassioned plea, "I am so crazy in love with you that I will come all the way to where you are, to be flesh of your flesh, bone of your bone."

God suffers alongside us, but God is not victimized by suffering. This is what the Resurrection makes clear. Jesus' resurrection after his death was the most profound incident of God making a way when there is no way. In Jesus, God overcomes the hopelessness that typically accompanies suffering by freely experiencing it and then bearing it away. In other words, God suffers with a purpose, to reconcile us to God's self. The resurrection of Jesus Christ shows us that God achieves this purpose through suffering. So suffering and even death do not have the final word. They cannot derail God's plan for the world or for you.

Once a father was walking in the woods with his son. As they walked along, the father accidentally stepped on an ant den. His young son saw that many were hurt or killed. Overcome with pity, the little boy knelt down and studied the quivering insects. "Isn't there anything we can do for these poor ants?" "No, nothing," replied his father. Yet, as the child pondered the ants' suffering, the father added, "If only I could somehow shrink myself down to their world and become an ant myself." As unlikely as it seems, this is what God has done for us. We can learn to trust a God who would do that.

FINDING YOUR PURPOSE

*"Earth's crammed with heaven, And every common bush
afire with God: But only he who sees, takes off his shoes.
The rest sit round it, and pluck blackberries."*
Elizabeth Barrett Browning

Near the end of his life, Moses stood before the people he had led out of Egypt, the people he had led for forty years. He shared with them a final word of advice. His words took on a dramatic intensity: "I call heaven and earth to witness against you today that I have before you life and death, blessings and curses. Choose life" (Deuteronomy 30:19). The great message is that we are given true freedom. Not only are we permitted to turn away from God and the promise of an authentic life, we are also given the freedom to turn toward them.

Your choice simplifies the search for meaning and purpose in life. It is the decision to live in such a way that you find your place within God's plan for peace, justice, and love. Discovering your purpose in life is really just becoming yourself. Rather than listening to those external voices who tell you who you are supposed to be, it is listening to an inner voice to discover the person God created you to be. In an old Jewish tale, Rabbi Zusya, an old man nearing the end of his life, said, "In the coming world, they will not ask me, 'Why were you not Moses?' They will ask me, 'Why were you not Zusya?'" You are not meant to go around looking for the burning bush, signaling that it is time to go and do great things. Instead, you are to look inside to your burning passions, to the gifts and inclinations that make you unique. Finding your purpose is discovering your authentic self. It is, as Frederick Buechner suggests, looking for "the place where your deep gladness meets the world's deep need."

Of course, discovering such a place requires us to pay attention to the leading of God's Spirit in our lives. As Lauren Winner reminds us, however, this can be difficult to do: "Sometimes, as in a great novel, you cannot see until you get to the end that God was leaving clues for you all along. Sometimes you wonder, 'How did I miss it?'"

At first, we are most keenly aware of our own searching, of our longing for answers, for meaning, for purpose. This is as it should be. Yet, over time, we become aware that our seeking is not a solitary pursuit but a response to a Seeker who has already found us. From Nicodemus looking for answers in the middle of the night to the woman at the well to Zacchaeus up a tree to a couple mourning the death of Jesus to Moses struggling to choose the one thing that will give him life, we have already learned that our search is not in vain, that our deep longing for God is met by God's yearning to be with us.

Six

HOW DOES GOD SPEAK TO ME?

Prayer is communion with God.

John Killinger

Now an angel of the Lord said to Philip, "Go south to the road—the desert road—that goes down from Jerusalem to Gaza." So he started out, and on his way he met an Ethiopian eunuch, an important official in charge of all the treasure of Candace, queen of the Ethiopians. This man had gone to Jerusalem to worship, and on his way home was sitting in his chariot reading the book of Isaiah the prophet. The Spirit told Philip, "Go to that chariot and stay near it."

Then Philip ran up to the chariot and heard the man reading Isaiah the prophet. "Do you understand what you are reading?" Philip asked.

"How can I," the eunuch said, "unless someone explains it to me?" So he invited Philip to come up and sit with him.

The eunuch was reading this passage of Scripture:

"He was led like a sheep to the slaughter,
   and as a lamb before the shearer is silent,

so he did not open his mouth.
In his humiliation he was deprived of justice.
Who can speak of his descendants?
For his life was taken from the earth."
The eunuch asked Philip, "Tell me, please, who is the prophet talking about, himself or someone else?" Then Philip began with that very passage of Scripture and told him the good news about Jesus. As they traveled along the road, they came to some water and the eunuch said, "Look, here is water. Why shouldn't I be baptized?" And he gave orders to stop the chariot. Then both Philip and the eunuch went down into the water and Philip baptized him. (Acts 8:26-38 NIV)

Why would an African official on the back of a chariot heading down a bumpy road be reading the ancient preacher Isaiah (Isaiah 53:7-8)? This official was a successful man, the chief financial officer of his nation, the head of his nation's federal reserve bank. We would expect him to be reading a financial spreadsheet, an internal audit report, or the *Wall Street Journal*. Instead, he was reading the Hebrew Scriptures. What was this Ethiopian official seeking? Why was this foreigner reading from the religious text of his host country?

If you are traveling from your home to a town you have never visited, you need a locator—a map or GPS. If you are putting together a child's bicycle, you need some guidance. If you are cooking a new food dish, you need a recipe. We all need assistance to get through life. Which map, what guidance, which recipe do we use if we are looking for God on our spiritual journeys along the way? How do we learn about God, Jesus Christ, and the Holy Spirit as we have described them in our first chapters?

In the middle of the Sinai Desert between Egypt and Israel, there is a large rock. On the sides of this rock, ancient people wrote graffiti. There are words of greeting; words of warning; and directions for travelers through the rocky, barren desert. Some of this graffiti is over two thousand years old. When you are traveling through a desert, such words can be a signpost promising you that you are on the right road and then guiding you in the right direction. The Bible is such a marker. It is a collection of stories by inquirers about inquirers for inquirers as they journey through life.

Many religions have their own sacred scriptures. For example, Jews use the Torah or Tanakh and Muslims follow the Koran. The adherents of each religion understand that their special writings are a cherished gift to a unique people. In today's culture, our "sacred" books are wireless electronic PDAs, cellular phones, global positioning units, and communicators that can answer every question we can possibly ask.

Christians' sacred book, the "Holy Bible," declares to God, "Your word is a lamp to my feet and a light to my path" (Psalm 119:105). Or, as Jesus said, "One does not live by bread alone, but by every word that comes from the mouth of God" (Matthew 4:4).

"The Bible has been the Book that has held together the fabric of western civilization."   *H. G. Wells*

Today, there are more Bibles than people in the United States. There are more Bibles than any other book in the world. But many people find the Bible a hard book to understand and think that the book seems full of "Thee's" and "Thou's." Go to any bookseller and you will find dozens of different translations in English. The places mentioned in the Bible are far away, and the customs seem strange. What about all those lists of dead people whose names no one can pronounce? Many of us get hazy about what is in the Bible: Did David or Goliath win the fight? (answer: David) What about Hercules and Xena, the warrior princess? Did these heroes make it into the Bible? (answer: no) Were Noah, Moses, and Jesus good friends or did they live at different times? (answer: different periods of history)

For Christians, however, the Bible provides answers and gives directions for the most basic spiritual questions we ask. It is "The Book" of the people who follow Jesus Christ. The Bible is our map, instruction sheet, and recipe book. As we read the Bible in public worship and in our private devotional lives, it helps us determine our faith and shows us how to live as followers of Jesus Christ. Christians are truly people of the Bible.

THE BIBLE: A DEFINITION

What is the Bible? The word *Bible* means "books" or "library." The Bible is a collection of sixty-six books written in a time span of over one thousand years of human history. Its writings occur in settings from Turkey to Israel to Egypt and beyond. This library includes books of history (Exodus), law (Leviticus), poetry (Psalms), prophecy (Isaiah), love letters (The Song of Solomon), international politics (First Kings), letters (Romans), biographies (Mark), and short stories (Jonah). Originally written in Hebrew, Aramaic, and Greek, the Bible, or parts of it, has now been translated into over two thousand languages. People have died protecting the book and translating it for other people to read. Europe split politically and religiously during the 1500s over the issue of whether the Bible could be translated into languages that ordinary people could understand. The Bible is the most studied book in the world—and the most misunderstood. Essentially, the Bible is a book inspired by God and written by people who have experienced God and want to share their experience with other people who are also seeking to experience God.

We hope that you have a copy of the Bible. Open the book to its table of contents. Notice that the Bible is divided between the Old and New Testaments. The Bible is further subdivided into sixty-six books; some versions of the Bible even have more books (called the Apocrypha), but that is a story for another day. Each book is also subdivided by chapters (the big numbers on most pages) and verses (the little numbers throughout the text). These numbers help us find our way through the Bible more quickly. For example, John 3:16 means the New Testament Gospel of John, chapter 3, verse 16.

The Old Testament, the first part of the Bible, is Jewish literature written before the birth of Jesus. The Old Testament includes stories about Creation, a great flood, the escape out of Egypt, David and Goliath, and lots of other dramatic narratives. We also hear of God establishing special relationships (we call this kind of relationship a "covenant") with people like Noah, Abraham and Sarah, Moses, and the people of Israel. The first part of the Bible also includes songs, poetry, prayers, wise sayings, prophecies about a coming liberator, and preachers calling for justice. This part of the Bible tells the dramatic story of a chosen and gifted people who lived through some of the most tumultuous periods of world history (from Creation to about three hundred years before the birth of Jesus). What Christians call the Old

Testament is also Jewish sacred Scripture. Christians believe these writings are truly inspired by God.

In addition, Christians hold the Bible in such high regard because we meet Jesus in this book. In the New Testament, written during the one hundred years after Jesus' life on earth, we discover God through the person of Jesus of Nazareth and the response of Jesus' contemporaries to him. The first four books of the New Testament—Matthew, Mark, Luke, and John—describe Jesus' birth, experiences, miracles, teachings, final days, and resurrection from the dead. The New Testament books then continue with the history of the early Christian church (Acts), letters of instructions to the first congregations (First Corinthians, for example), and a description of the culmination of history (Revelation). Because we believe that Jesus Christ reveals God most clearly, the New Testament is our definitive sacred writing from God, since it points women and men to Jesus.

> *"In his Word God does not deliver me a course of lectures in dogmatic theology, he does not submit to me or interpret for me the content of a confession of faith, but he makes himself accessible to me."*   *Emil Brunner*

Augustine, a fourth-century intellectual, discovered Jesus Christ through the Bible. Augustine was born of a pagan father and a Christian mother in northern Africa in the last years of the Roman Empire. A brilliant young man, he prepared to become a lawyer and then switched to the study of philosophy and rhetoric. He lived the rich life of a Roman intellectual and had a relationship with a mistress. Then, at age thirty in AD 386, Augustine had a transforming experience with God. This experience took place in a small garden in Milan, Italy, as he wrestled with

God about their relationship with each other. Here is part of Augustine's story:

"I went on talking…and weeping in the most intense bitterness of my broken heart. Suddenly I heard a voice from a house nearby—perhaps a voice of some boy or a girl, I do not know—singing over and over again, 'Pick it [the Bible] up and read, pick it up and read.' My expression immediately altered and I began to think hard whether children ordinarily repeated a ditty like this in any sort of game, but I could not recall ever having heard it anywhere else. I stemmed the flood of tears and rose to my feet, believing that this could be nothing other than a divine command to open the Book and read the first passage I chanced upon. I snatched it up, opened it and read in silence the passage on which my eyes first lighted: *Not in dissipation and drunkenness, not in debauchery and lewdness, not in arguing and jealousy; but put on the Lord Jesus Christ, and make not provision for the flesh or the gratification of your desires* [Romans 13:13-14]. I had no wish to read further, nor was there need. No sooner had I reached the end of the verse than the light of certainty flooded my heart and all dark shades of doubt fled away."

After his experience, Augustine returned to his hometown in North Africa and became a preacher, a teacher, and an author in the church.

The Bible is a key component of what we call the "Word of God." We mean by the "Word of God" that God reveals God's own self in the Bible and still speaks to us through this book. In the Bible, God's own words and mighty acts in human history were witnessed and heard, passed along orally, written down, and copied through thousands of years. The Holy Bible is the Spirit-filled, living, dynamic, ever-unfolding presence of God among us. In the Bible, God has authoritatively spoken and continues to speak to guide our faith and practice.

Christians do not worship the Bible, however. For us, the "Word of God" took flesh in Jesus Christ (John 1) and the Holy Spirit continues to speak God's Word to us in multiple ways, such as in preaching. As one biblical author wrote, "Indeed, the word of God is living and active, sharper than any two-edged sword, piercing until it divides soul from spirit, joints from marrow; it is able to judge the thoughts and intentions of the heart" (Hebrews 4:12). Christians are careful not to worship the written word of the Bible, as if God stopped speaking two thousand years ago, but instead use the Bible to help us follow the living Word, Jesus Christ.

BASIC QUESTIONS

Do we believe every word in the Bible? Are all these biblical stories historically accurate? Christians believe that every word in Scripture comes from God and was written down and transmitted by faithful human beings who were in close relationship with God. Bruce Feiler writes, "It's a living, breathing entity unencumbered by the sterilization of time. If anything, it's an ongoing narrative: stories that begin in the sand, get entrenched in stone, pass down through families, and play themselves out in the lives of residents and visitors who traverse its lines nearly five thousand years after they were first etched into memory." The Bible especially describes our own intimate relationship with God.

Yet, sometimes we ask more of the Bible than the Bible is able to provide. While the Bible describes the universe, it is not a science book. While the Bible is placed in history and contains historical facts, it is not a history book.

While the Bible looks into the future, the Bible is not a book of precise predictions. While the Bible gives lots of advice, the Bible is not a rule book. The Bible is not a self-help book, nor is it full of quick and easy answers. Fundamentally, the Bible is a profound mapping of the way. Let's look, for example, at the Creation story. The first chapter of the Bible, Genesis 1, says that God created the universe in six days and that God rested on the seventh day. Does the Bible, therefore, mean that God created the world in six twenty-four hour days? Are modern scientific understandings of the universe false? Should we reject modern astronomy, physics, biology, anthropology, and paleontology as unsound? No. Genesis declares first and foremost that God created everything and called it good. Genesis was never intended to be a scientific explanation of "how" God created the universe and life within it. Genesis explains "who" created everything and "why" God did so. It may be that God created the universe via the "Big Bang," and life developed slowly over time. Or not. We are still learning how the universe and life were formed. But Christians are certain that God was at the beginning, set the universe on a good course that has continued until today, and still watches over and intervenes throughout the universe.

God created human beings with inquisitive minds, good teachers, and our own set of experiences. When we read the Bible, we must ask if the text is reasonable based on everything we know, if collective human wisdom through the centuries proves its worthiness, and then test the Bible against our own experience. While the Bible is our final authority, we also must ask our best scholars what it means, talk about it with other Christians, and then evaluate Scripture by how we have experienced God.

Are there contradictions in the Bible? Does it say one thing in one book and then something else in another book? The answer is that any library that contains sixty-six different books written in different times by different people in different places and dealing with different situations will at times tell the same truth in different ways. Since no two people ever see one accident in exactly the same way, we should not assume that all the biblical authors experienced God in exactly the same way. For example, at the beginning of the Bible, in the first two chapters of Genesis, there are two very different descriptions of Creation. In Genesis 1, plants and animals are created before man and woman; but in Genesis 2, human beings are created before plants and animals. Do these two versions mean that the universe was created two times or that one story is right and the other narrative is wrong? A more plausible theory is that these stories are two different but equally faithful ways of describing the same event. In addition, in some places the Bible seems to encourage polygamy, slavery, and the inequality of men and women, all of which the Bible itself also opposes in other places. In the subsequent generations since the time of writing, it has taken clear thoughts, collective understandings, and a range of experiences to determine that the biblical witness opposes polygamy, slavery, and sexism.

At its heart, there are no contradictions in the Bible. The Bible fundamentally tells us about the truth of our relationship with God, how God and people meet, ways we fail God, where God's unfailing love reclaims us, and how to live moral lives. One of the New Testament authors describes to a group of Christians the primary purpose of the Bible this way: "From childhood you have known the sacred writings that are able to instruct you for salvation through faith in Christ Jesus. All scripture is inspired by God and is useful for teaching, for reproof, for correction, and for training in righteousness, so that everyone who belongs to God may be proficient, equipped for every good work" (2 Timothy 3:15-17). The Bible contains everything we need to know about how we can be in relationship with God.

In other words, the Bible does not operate as a science book, history book, or predictor of the future. The Bible operates like a magnet, a compass, an electrical conductor, a window, and a key helping us understand God. God through the Bible draws us to God, points us in the right direction, conveys wisdom to us; opens our eyes to see Jesus Christ; and unlocks the doors of our minds, hearts, and lives. The Bible helps us know which roads to take in our journeys along the way.

IS THE BIBLE STILL USEFUL?

The Bible is about real life, moral truths, and our relationship with God. Here is an example of how the Bible reveals God to us:

Once upon a time there was a man named Job. Job was a good man, who was very rich and had a great family. But disaster after disaster hit Job. Through no fault of his own and despite his righteousness, Job got sick, his children died, his property was taken away, and his friends deserted him. Job, covered with dirt and sores, was reduced to sitting by the side of the road. In his fragile condition, Job complained to his friends, argued with his wife, and challenged God to tell him why he, a good man, had to suffer. While his friends told Job that his failures were his own fault and chastised him for challenging God, God listened to Job and talked with him.

God told Job that there were answers to his questions but that Job would never understand the answers. By the end of the Book of Job, Job still had no clear answer about why he was suffering. But Job knew that God had not deserted him, and Job rejoiced in his new and stronger relationship with God.

We all have had "Job experiences." Every one of us has suffered—many times through no fault of our own. We get sick, a family member dies, we lose a job, or a relationship ends. We ask questions and seek answers: "Why me?" "Why now?" "What did I do to deserve this?" In the Bible through Job we discover that God is with us in good times and in bad times. While we will never understand why bad things happen to good people, the Bible encourages us to debate our situation with our friends and God vigorously. In the midst of pain, challenging God with our toughest questions is appropriate. Yet, in the end, the Bible is clear that God never deserts us. Even if we do not find all the answers we want, God is always there for us.

Every biblical story, if we look carefully, illumines our lives, declares to us who God is, and describes how Jesus Christ works in our lives. As we walk through the Bible, we meet wonderful characters, experience awesome stories, ask profound questions, and hear challenging answers. The Bible is holy because it is from God and because it is about our relationship to God in the most profound ways.

HOW CAN I USE THE BIBLE?

"The meditation of Scripture centers on internalizing and personalizing the passage. The written word becomes a living word addressed to you." Richard Foster

If our description of the Bible intrigues you, how do you start reading this book? How can you start using the Bible as a map in your journey? It is hard just to pick up the Bible at random and start reading. The words may be difficult, and your mind may wander. You need a plan. Start with an easy-to-understand modern translation. We recommend that you consider either the New Revised Standard Version (NRSV) or the New International Version (NIV).

Begin reading one of the Gospels (one of the first four New Testament books, which describe the life of Jesus), such as the Gospel of Mark, which tells the story of Jesus from his baptism to his resurrection from the dead. After Mark, read the Acts of the Apostles, the story of the earliest church and how the good news of Jesus Christ spread around the world. You may then want to explore the poetry of the Book of Psalms, in the middle of the Bible, and then read some Old Testament stories like the Book of Job.

As you read, ask yourself three questions, each of which can be answered very simply or with a great deal of discussion and depth:

1. What does the Bible say? For example, what is the first chapter of Genesis about? (Answer: God created the universe and called it good.)

2. What does this passage say to me? (Answer: God created me and called me good.)

3. What does this passage expect of me? (Answer: To respect all creation and all people as being created by God and having sacred worth.)

Prepare to be startled by what you find. When you read the Bible, it will make demands on you—not just the act of reading it, but what it says to you. A ubiquitous quotation is attributed to Martin Luther, the German monk who began a church reform movement five hundred years ago: "The Bible is alive, it speaks to me; it has feet, it runs after me; it has hands, it lays hold of me." Almost any Bible story can lay hold of you also.

Often, private Bible study is best. Find a quiet place, read a passage out loud, and ask the three questions: What does the Bible say? What does this passage say to me? What does this passage expect of me? Just five minutes of Bible study a few days a week will get you off to a great start.

In addition to private study, you may also consider a group Bible study. Being led by an experienced Bible teacher in a congregation, in someone's home, or at work and studying with a group of other inquirers will reveal more about the Bible story than you could ever imagine. Everyone brings a unique perspective to each story, and you will learn more together than anyone can learn alone.

READ IT

Do you remember the story about Philip and the African official with which we began this chapter? After Philip got into the chariot, he explained to the official that the passage about the sheep who was slaughtered without protest was a story about Jesus. Philip then explained that he knew Jesus, that Jesus had been unjustly crucified, that Jesus had been resurrected, and that Jesus was still alive. At the end of the conversation, the African official asked Philip to baptize him and accept him as a follower of Jesus Christ so that he could continue his journey. On that day, talking about Scripture, the official became the first African follower of Jesus Christ.

Consider today reading the Bible itself. Pick it up and try it. God is trying to speak to you through it.

Seven

IF I DON'T FEEL LOST, WHY DO I NEED TO BE FOUND?

God does not wait for us to have our spiritual acts together before reaching out to us and seeking relationship with us.

Kimberly Dunnam Reisman

Jesus [said], "There was a man who had two sons. The younger one said to his father, 'Father, give me my share of the estate.' So [the father] divided his property between [his sons].

"Not long after that, the younger son got together all he had, set off for a distant country and there squandered his wealth in wild living. After he had spent everything, there was a severe famine in that whole country, and he began to be in need. So he went and hired himself out to a citizen of that country, who sent him to his fields to feed pigs. He longed to fill his stomach with the [food] that the pigs were eating, but no one gave him anything.

"When he came to his senses, he said, 'How many of my father's hired men have food to spare, and here I am starving to death! I will set out and go back to my father and say to him: Father, I have sinned against heaven and against you. I am no longer worthy to be called your son; make me like one of your hired men.' So he got up and went to his father.

"But while he was still a long way off, his father saw him and was filled with compassion for him; he ran to his son, threw his arms around him and kissed him.

"The son said to him, 'Father, I have sinned against heaven and against you. I am no longer worthy to be called your son.'

"But the father said to his servants, 'Quick! Bring the best robe and put it on him. Put a ring on his finger and sandals on his feet. Bring the fattened calf and kill it. Let's have a feast and celebrate. For this son of mine was dead and is alive again; he was lost and is found.' So they began to celebrate."

(Luke 15:11-24 NIV)

Why did the younger son run away? He had everything he could need: a warm bed, food to eat, lifelong friends, plenty of hired help, and a father who loved him. Yet, this son set off on a journey to a foreign land, lost everything, and found himself homeless and hungry. The good news in this biblical story is that people who are lost can be found by God. These people, when they find themselves at a crossroad, choose the right road to take and discover the outreaching arms of Jesus Christ.

ARE YOU SAVED?

Have you ever been approached on the street or at work or in the mall and asked, "Are you saved?" Have you received a pamphlet through the mail or found a note in a public place that asked, "If you died today, where would you be?" What are these people talking about?

Christians believe that when we are lost, God in Jesus Christ through the Holy Spirit makes a decisive, lifelong, transforming change in our lives. We believe that, as in the story of the wayward son, Jesus Christ invites us and empowers us to turn around and return home, to walk down the right road and head in the right direction, in other words, to be found. Without Jesus Christ guiding our lives, we may be rascals like the younger son, or we may be sincere, well-meaning, and good citizens; but we are not yet fully what God created us to be. Jesus Christ wants all people to understand themselves as God's chosen children (John 1:12). Claiming that we are children of God, being followers of Jesus Christ, and entering into a transforming relationship with God, who created us and welcomes us home, is what we mean by "being saved" or "salvation."

A DEFINITION OF SALVATION

The word *salvation* has a variety of meanings. Salvation means that God in Jesus Christ through the Holy Spirit is working in our lives to make us well, whole, and strong in our relationship with God. This new life Jesus Christ offers us involves balance and harmony in our bodies, minds, and spirits; it is like an infant being held by and clinging to her or his mother. When we are uncertain about the meaning of life, when we have fundamental needs that are not being met, when our relationships with other people are broken, when we feel isolated from God, when we question the way on which we are traveling, Jesus Christ offers comfort, reconciliation, and direction. Salvation is a lifelong relationship with Jesus Christ. When we enter into that relationship, we receive the assurance that God loves us and we gain the ability to love God and other people completely. When we enter that relationship with Jesus Christ, we are clearly on our way home.

In *This Is Christianity*, Maxie Dunnam writes that Christians in Africa have translated the English word *salvation* as "God took our heads out." This translation comes from the slave trade in Africa. When Africans were captured for slavery, the overlords bolted an iron collar around the neck of each slave. The slaves would then wear their collars of bondage as they traveled to slave boats, made the Middle Passage to North America, and were sold in the New World. The only hope for each slave was to have her or his head taken out of the collar of oppression. In this context, God in Jesus Christ through the cross and resurrection saves us from our bondage to sin and death. As the Bible declares, "For God so loved the world that God gave God's only Son, so that everyone who believes in Jesus may not perish but may have eternal life" (John 3:16; author's translation).

SALVATION AS RELATIONSHIP

Salvation is not a thing we possess; it is a relationship we enter. For example, Christian salvation does not mean simply that we may wear a cross pendant—it means that we have a continuing relationship with Jesus Christ. Compare salvation to the love between two people. Love between two people is not an object they can put on a chain or place in their pocket or wear on their finger. Instead, love is the name of a deep and abiding relationship with another person. Sometimes we can identify the moment love happens—love at first sight. Sometimes we realize that we are in love only after a long period of friendship. Love can exist between a mother and her child, between two friends, or in a marriage. Because another person loves me, I can love that person; and the two of us are better together than either of us was separately.

In a similar way, *salvation* is the word that describes our relationship with Jesus Christ. Salvation is a relationship in which we experience to our very depths that Jesus Christ loves us, and then we offer ourselves back to him. Just as the runaway son was never outside his father's love, neither are we. Salvation involves every aspect of our lives. Salvation is about a living relationship with God here and now. Salvation involves how we care for ourselves, how we care for other people, and how we care for our world. Salvation is also about our continuing relationship with Jesus Christ even after we die.

SALVATION AS JOURNEY

As we pointed out in the introduction, Lewis Carroll's Cheshire Cat says that if you don't know where you are going, any road will take you there. But at most of life's crossroad, there are worse roads and better roads to take.

Christians describe an intimate, personal relationship with Jesus Christ as a journey similar to the one the runaway son experienced. Throughout the ages, Christians have used this journey metaphor: from Dante Alighieri's *The Divine Comedy*, describing his journey to heaven, to Geoffrey Chaucer's *Canterbury Tales*, telling of pilgrims on their way to a sacred site in Canterbury, England, to John Bunyan's *Pilgrim's Progress*, allegorizing about Christian life, to Charles Dickens' *A Christmas Carol*, detailing Ebenezer Scrooge's life on Christmas Eve.

On this journey, which we call the Christian life, we move closer and closer to Jesus Christ. This journey covers many roads with numerous twists and turns. Many different traveling companions join us. As we travel, there are strange bypaths and frequent stops for rest and renewal. Sometimes we move forward in a straight line. Sometimes we travel in the opposite direction. Sometimes the journey feels like a roller coaster with slow ascents, rapid descents, and unexpected loops. Throughout this journey we have the freedom to stop, get off the road, or head back whence we came. This journey takes a whole lifetime. And while the final goal is life everlasting, salvation also involves living in a loving relationship with God and other people every day. The journey is just as important as the destination.

All of us have been on a spiritual journey throughout our lives. Jesus Christ has invited every one of us to be in a special relationship with him. This invitation comes as a gracious offer, to which we then respond, "We love God because God first loved us" (1 John 4:19; author's translation). Jesus' life, teachings, death, and resurrection are our clearest examples of God's love. Jesus' invitation includes a gracious promise. As Jesus said, "I came that [you] may have life, and have it abundantly" (John 10:10). When we accept the invitation to join Jesus Christ on the journey, we are blessed now and forever.

Above all, Christians believe that our journey of salvation is a journey that Jesus Christ initiates. Just like God coming to the world when and where God was least expected—in the baby born in Bethlehem—and Jesus overcoming sin on the cross and overwhelming death through his resurrection, God is in control of each journey. God's love for us does not depend upon whether we act good or come to worship every Sunday or give generously to the poor or pray constantly or read the Bible daily or take part in a program. Instead, according to Jesus, God is running toward us faster than we are running toward God. On each step of our journey there is reciprocity: God speaks and we respond. God does not save us without our consent. God and we need each other. But throughout this journey God has prepared the road, is always watching for our return home, and is eager to run toward us.

A Christian song, "Amazing Grace," makes this same observation. John Newton had gone to sea as a young cabin boy, eventually becoming the captain of an English ship that carried slaves to the New World. As Newton began to reflect upon his life, he read the Bible and occasionally attended worship. Newton ended up as a priest in the Church of England. In this hymn Newton wrote that he did not find God but God found him:

> Amazing grace! How sweet the sound,
> that saved a wretch like me!
> I once was lost, but now am found;
> was blind, but now I see.

Newton understood that in his journey God sought him tirelessly and insistently.

THE WAY OF SALVATION

There are a number of way stations in our journey of salvation. While we may number the steps of the journey or give each stopping place a name or describe the journey in one particular style, no two people ever take the same steps. The way may be linear or circular or spiraling. We may experience our journey with God in many different ways, and we may have to revisit a number of the sites. On every journey along the way, there are always new experiences, growth, and ultimately joy.

> *"God must, in some way or other, make room, hollowing us out and emptying us, if God is finally to penetrate into us. And in order to assimilate us, God must break the molecules of our being so as to re-cast and re-model us."*
> *Pierre Teilhard de Chardin*

One way to describe this journey is by naming four of the primary way stations:

Way Station One: God Seeking Us → Our Listening
Way Station Two: God Convicting Us → Our Asking for Forgiveness
Way Station Three: God Embracing Us → Our Trusting
Way Station Four: God Empowering Us → Our Living Faithfully

Let's describe these four major locations or moments in our journey:

WAY STATION ONE: GOD SEEKING US → OUR LISTENING

Our journey with Jesus Christ begins before we are even aware that we are on a journey. This first stage is a gentle, quiet, in-breaking love for us; it is the way station of God's initiating love. For the father with the younger son, the father's love for his son was absolute. The father loved his son from the moment of his birth and certainly before his son could reciprocate that love. Even when the younger son wanted his inheritance early in Luke 15, the father willingly divided his property and gave the younger son his share. And so God loves us and guides us before we ever love God. Our response to this love is to listen and say, "Thank you."

Take, for example, Moses, the man who led the Hebrews out of slavery in Egypt. Although Moses was seemingly unaware of God's presence in his life until he was almost eighty years of age, God was with Moses throughout his life. God watched over Moses when he was born into a slave family, when midwives saved him from the Egyptian king's soldiers, when his mother put him in a basket in the river Nile to hide him, when the king's daughter rescued Moses from the river, when he was reared in the royal household, when Moses fled from a murder charge, and when Moses found a new family in the Sinai Desert. Only late in his life, through a burning bush, did Moses learn the name of God. God had been a part of Moses' journey from the moment of Moses' conception, and God had some magnificent plans for him (see Exodus).

God loves each of us from the moment of our creation and seeks us before we know God's name or consciously seek God. Jesus Christ starts a love song and sings the first words. At this stage God may speak only in soft whispers. Sometimes we are too busy, too distracted, or speak too much to hear, but Jesus Christ's whispers are there, and God gives us ears to hear.

Have you heard Jesus Christ whispering to you to consider a relationship with him? Jesus Christ may speak to you in many ways during this early stage in your relationship with God: through a family member, a spouse, friends, the Bible and prayer. Jesus Christ may speak to you through situations in your life: your parent dies, your child asks a religious question and you do not know the answer, there are difficulties in your marriage, a close friendship collapses, you lose your job, or airplanes hit office towers. When you realize that you have no one else to turn to, Jesus Christ is speaking softly to you. Sometimes you may listen, and sometimes you may not; but Jesus Christ keeps speaking. He keeps singing a love song.

Most often, like the runaway son who fell on hard times or like Moses tending sheep in the desert, you may not even know God is moving in your life until after the fact. It was only after the runaway had wasted his fortune and was forced into the lowest form of manual labor that he became aware of his father's love. As you look back on your life, you may discover Jesus Christ working during every moment of every day of your life. In these moments, you may discover that God has been opening your eyes, ears, and heart to be in a relationship with Jesus Christ. Your only response to this quiet, persistent love is to say, "Thank you!" As you begin to put a little bit of yourself into the relationship, you are on the way. This is the beginning of the way of salvation.

WAY STATION TWO:
GOD CONVICTING US → OUR ASKING FOR FORGIVENESS

Author/activist Will Campbell recalls that during his participation in the Civil Rights Movement, a friend challenged him to define Christianity in ten words or less. As Campbell considered all the people involved in that turbulent era, from white racists to silent Christians to black radicals, he responded, "We're all bastards, but God loves us anyway."

When the runaway son discovered how far he was from home and that he was starving while his father's servants were well fed, he returned home. This was the way station of repentance. When the son understood how badly he had failed his father and himself, he realized it was time to say, "I'm sorry."

All of us ultimately know that we are not the people God created us to be. As we continue on our spiritual journeys, there are moments in our lives when Jesus Christ causes us to become discontent with our status quo. We become ill at ease with the way things are in our lives. We question our achievements and values. We recognize that we may wear masks we do not like, that we engage in activities that do not bring us fulfillment, and that the meaning of our lives is unclear. All of us have on occasion sold ourselves to our jobs, our family, our possessions, drugs, sex, and many other lesser gods.

Christians believe that all of us fail, fail often, and fail miserably. No matter how hard we try to do what is right, we hit potholes and roadblocks in our journey. Even when we know the right thing to do, we do the opposite. The God-shaped hole in our lives seems to get bigger. At these moments, when we understand that our lives are self-centered, dis-ordered, and dis-eased, when we acknowledge our failure and see how far we have traveled down the wrong path, Jesus Christ helps us. At these moments, we may say like the Old Testament preacher, "Woe is me! I am lost, for I am a [person] of unclean lips, and I live among a people of unclean lips" (Isaiah 6:5). God does not just tell us that we are guilty and convict us of our failures, however. Through Jesus Christ, God offers to us at this way station the freedom to choose. God has gifted us from our creation with the power to decide freely for ourselves which god we will follow, which path we will select. When we are at the crossroad, we can and must choose which road to follow.

When you recognize that you are starving while your father's servants are feasting, the good news is that you can turn toward home. You can say to Jesus Christ, "I'm sorry. Forgive me." In the movie *She Wore a Yellow Ribbon*, John Wayne as Captain Nathan Brittles said of apologizing, "It's a sign of weakness." However, we believe that apologizing to God and asking for relief is a sign of strength. At this moment, God forgives your mistakes and washes you clean to begin life anew. Your failures are forgotten. As Jesus said to the adulterous woman, "Neither do I condemn you. Go your way, and from now on do not sin again" (John 8:11). While you may fail over and over and need to say "I'm sorry" again and again, God in Jesus Christ gives you power over your wayward thoughts and deeds.

WAY STATION THREE:
GOD EMBRACING US → OUR TRUSTING

At the very moment of his deepest despair and failure, the runaway son discovered his greatest joy. Even while the son was at some distance from his home, his father, who had been on constant watch, saw his son, rushed to him, embraced him, and restored the son into the household. Turning to Jesus Christ is not turning in a 360-degree circle but turning in the opposite direction, that is, making a 180-degree turn. At this stage, you recognize your limitations and say to Jesus Christ, "Redirect me."

One illustration of this moment occurred in the life of a man called Saul. Within a few years after the resurrection of Jesus Christ, many Jewish people were following Christ. Saul, a zealous, young Jew, persecuted people who followed Jesus. Saul was sent from Jerusalem to Damascus to arrest some of the new Christians. On his way, Saul (whom we know as the apostle Paul) had a dramatic experience with Jesus Christ. This is Paul's account from Acts 22:

> "While I was on my way and approaching Damascus, about noon a great light from heaven suddenly shone about me. I fell to the ground and heard a voice saying to me, 'Saul, Saul, why are you persecuting me?' I answered, 'Who are you, Lord?' Then he said to me, 'I am Jesus of Nazareth whom you are persecuting.' Now those people who were with me saw the light but did not hear the voice of the one who was speaking to me. I asked, 'What am I to do, Lord?' The Lord said to me, 'Get up and go to Damascus; there you will be told everything that has been assigned to you to do.' Since I could not see because of the brightness of that light, those persons who were with me took my hand and led me to Damascus."
>
> (Acts 22:6-11)

When Saul arrived in Damascus, the followers of Jesus were afraid of him. Hadn't he come to persecute them? Was this a trick? But one of the Christians was willing to trust that Jesus Christ had brought Saul to them. And so the story continues:

> "A certain Ananias, who was a devout man according to the law and well spoken of by all the Jews living there, came to me. . . . He said, 'Brother Saul, regain your sight!' In that very hour I regained my sight and saw him. Then he said, 'The God of our

ancestors has chosen you to know [God's] will, to see the Righteous One and to hear his own voice; for you will be his witness to all the world of what you have seen and heard. And now why do you delay? Get up, be baptized, and have your sins washed away, calling on his name.'"

(Acts 22:12-16)

After his redirection, Saul began a ministry to non-Jews, especially in Asia Minor and Europe, that began a spiritual renewal of the Roman Empire. Most Christian stories of such redirection, however, are not as dramatic as Paul's.

When you come to the way station of being embraced by God and trusting in Jesus Christ's guidance, you are saved from something and saved for something (Colossians 1:13-14). You gain an assurance that you are saved from your inclination to put yourself first. You turn your back on your most persistent enemy, the evil in you. And you are saved to follow Jesus Christ. The message of salvation is a two-sided coin: uncovering your failures and opening your eyes to new paths (2 Corinthians 5:17). You trust Jesus Christ to forgive your failures and make you a new person.

WAY STATION FOUR:
GOD EMPOWERING US → OUR LIVING FAITHFULLY

The final stage in our journey with Jesus Christ, the way station of spiritual growth, we can only speculate about in regard to the runaway son. We do not know what happened after his father welcomed him home. Did the son become a faithful child, working each day in the fields? Did he try to repay the money he had lost? Did he give generously to strangers in his country? Did he never leave home again? We do not know. If the son truly wanted to celebrate his father's love, surely he would be a different person for the rest of his life, not out of debt and guilt, but as a way to honor his father's steadfast love.

Having heard Jesus Christ's whispers and listened, having felt God's judgment and repented, having been embraced by God and trusted in Jesus Christ, what does the final stage of the journey of salvation look like? Jesus Christ is not looking just for people to make one decision at one crossroad; he is looking for people to become lifelong followers who imitate his life. Jesus Christ invites everyone who has made it this far in the journey to be a faithful member of the community of fellow travelers and to live in this world as he guides them. At this stage, our response to Jesus Christ is, "Re-form me. Re-shape me. Re-mold me." At this stage in our journey, we discover that we become like Jesus Christ, loving God with all our heart, soul, and strength (Deuteronomy 6:4-5). Our life, our values, our goals, and our motives change. We discover that the meaning of life comes from loving God and serving other people.

At this final stage of the journey, the Holy Spirit works within you to help you grow in your love of God and other people. Your goal is to grow to be more like Jesus (Ephesians 4:13) and to be a new person (2 Corinthians 5:17). Jesus Christ wants you to be complete in your love of God and neighbor; anything less is less than God's desire for you. While the birth of a child is a foundational event, the life that follows any birth is even more diverse, exciting, and rich. The Bible uses many other images to represent such spiritual growth at this stage in our walk with Jesus Christ, such as growing wheat, constructing a house, or going on a journey.

THE CONTINUING JOURNEY OF SALVATION

"It seems to me a lifelong endeavor to try to live the life of a Christian."
                                                    Maya Angelou

As in any good journey, the journey never completely ends. As in any good relationship, the relationship never ceases. There are always more surprises, more experiences, and more opportunities in the days to come. Our relationship with Jesus Christ will never reach a plateau and stay there. Walking with Jesus Christ means that every day we must want to be more self-giving, to seek more inclusive justice, to care even more for other people, and to show God's love. We continue this journey, knowing that nothing, not even death itself, can separate us from God's love in Jesus Christ.

"We cannot forget the power of Christian conversion, that radical decision to turn away from sin and back to God, which reaches to the depths of a person's soul and can work extraordinary change."
                                                    Pope John Paul II

This journey with Jesus Christ through all these way stations is itself salvation. Salvation involves a lifetime of inward experiences and outward expressions of love. You know God through Jesus Christ in your heart and head, and you serve God through Jesus Christ with your lips, hands, and feet. You walk with Jesus Christ, and you walk beside other people who also follow Jesus Christ. What is important is not that you have any one particular experience or that you visit all four way stations in any one sequence but that you begin to live in relationship with God through Jesus Christ, who loves us and offers us love, forgiveness, confidence, and new life. What is required of us is a willingness to listen, to kneel, to trust, and to serve. The result is a personal transformation, sometimes in an instant and sometimes over a lifetime. We want to be like Jesus, to be his friend, to trust him, and to follow him. As Paul wrote, "It is no longer I who live, but it is Christ who lives in me" (Galatians 2:20).

IS EVERY JOURNEY THE SAME?

Every person comes into a relationship with Jesus Christ in a different way. Various translations of the Bible use a variety of expressions to name the beginning of a spiritual life (John 3:3): "born from above" (NRSV) or "born again" (KJV; NIV) Another word for this experience of redirection toward Jesus Christ is *conversion*. Every conversion is unique. No one pattern fits everyone. Conversions may be dramatic or quiet, emotional or intellectual, exciting or plain, instantaneous or gradual, personal or corporate, the result of a single crisis or of a long process, or a combination of all of the above. Conversion involves a constellation of factors, with many stars and configurations. Some people have many conversion experiences, and other people have one conversion that takes a whole lifetime to unfold. While the famous evangelist Billy Graham can name the place, day, and time of his redirection, his wife, Ruth, said that she was always a Christian, from the day of her birth.

The earliest followers of Jesus had various ways of being in relationship with him. Peter, the fisherman who first heard Jesus' invitation to follow, had no instantaneous experience when his life changed. Instead, Peter had a sequence of mundane and dramatic experiences along the way with Jesus, including catching fish, sharing meals, conversing along the road, watching Jesus ascend into heaven, and other events throughout their three-year time together. Then there was Timothy, a New Testament traveling teacher. Timothy received an inherited faith from his grandmother (Lois) and his mother (Eunice) and then shared what he learned from these women with other people. Every story and every journey along the way and through the way stations is different.

What is common in all these redirections or conversions, however, is that each life-changing experience is initiated by God directly engaging one individual and then that individual responds directly back to God. Conversion always begins with God whispering to you, challenging you, embracing you, empowering you, reaching out for you, running for you, and calling you. God wants to get back what God created: every one of us. There is a need for every individual to hear the voice of God and to make a personal decision to follow or not to follow Jesus Christ.

Christians who know Jesus Christ—his story, his teachings, his death and resurrection, and his continuing relationship with us—believe that Jesus Christ is the very presence of God for us and that Jesus Christ calls us to follow him. While we respect the beliefs of other people, we also have a steadfast allegiance to the Savior who reached out and still reaches out to us. It is Jesus Christ's story that we proclaim and by whose name we live. Jesus Christ is the one who has joined us in our journey, and if we want to be in relationship with God, we have to walk with Jesus Christ.

AN INVITATION

Bob Dylan wrote the song "You Gotta Serve Somebody" during a period of intense spiritual reflection as he considered his own spiritual journey. Dylan realized that whatever our station in life, we have to serve somebody. So, whom are you going to serve? On which road are you going to travel?

HOW CAN I BEGIN AN INTENTIONAL JOURNEY WITH JESUS CHRIST?

"In making a choice or in coming to a decision, only one thing is really important—to seek and to find what God called me to at this time in my life." Ignatius of Loyola

Being a Christian means following Jesus Christ. How does that happen? Remember the inquirer in our first chapter, Nicodemus? Nicodemus was a good man who was looking for the meaning of life. Nicodemus probably fasted twice a week, prayed in the Temple in Jerusalem, gave his money away generously, and even taught at the religious academy. Yet with all these good deeds, he was still looking for direction in his journey. Jesus said to Nicodemus, "You must be born from above" (John 3:7).

Because from the moment of birth all human beings are on a spiritual journey, the question is not "When will you begin your walk with Jesus Christ?"—Jesus Christ has always been walking beside you. Rather, the major question is "Are you ready to begin an intentional, deliberate, and disciplined journey with Jesus Christ?" You have to choose which road to travel. Christians are the people who choose to walk along the way with Jesus Christ. How do you decide? How can you begin?

For each person, the answer is different. In the New Testament and throughout history, each of Jesus' followers came to him differently. Stories of redirection toward Jesus often have more differences than similarities. There is no simple formula, no cookie cutter recipe, no one road map, and no magic words. But all Christians have made a choice to follow Jesus Christ.

Can you choose to follow Jesus Christ today? Of course you can. Should you choose today? That is for you to decide. But if you want to walk down Jesus' path, one way to go is simply to say several very simple words to Jesus Christ. These words parallel the four "way stations" in the spiritual journey. They begin as follows:

1. "Thank you, God," for your love. Jesus said to Nicodemus, "God so loved the world that God gave God's only Son, so that everyone who believes in Jesus Christ may not perish but may have eternal life" (John 3:16; author's translation). You, too, have to acknowledge God as your loving Parent. Open your eyes, ears, and heart to see Jesus Christ coming to you and embracing you.

2. "I'm sorry" that I have not been following your way. Jesus began his ministry by telling everyone, "Turn around and believe in the good news" (Mark 1:15; author's translation). If you have been walking down another road, you must admit that you have not been walking with Jesus Christ.

3. "Redirect me," and help me follow Jesus Christ in every step I take. As Peter, another New Testament writer, said, "Follow in his [Jesus'] steps" (1 Peter 2:21) and "for you were going astray like sheep, but now you have returned to the shepherd" (1 Peter 2:25). Say to Jesus Christ, "Jesus, be my companion and guide; point me in the right direction."

4. "Let's start" the journey today. As Paul said to some early Christians, "Now is the day of salvation" (2 Corinthians 6:2). Jesus Christ can become your guide today. "If you confess with your lips that Jesus is Lord and believe in your heart that God raised [Jesus] from the dead, you will be saved" (Romans 10:9). You may choose a new road to travel right now.

It is that simple.

These four phrases—Thank you, I'm sorry, Redirect me, Let's start—may take the form of a private conversation with God, such as,

"O loving God, I'm sorry about the roads I have traveled. I want to travel with Jesus today. Amen."

or

"Almighty God, I've made some wrong turns and am far from where I need to be. Jesus, guide me now. Amen."

or

"Jesus, I'm sorry. Why don't you take over now? Amen."

These four steps may also take place during a conversation with a Christian. Just ask someone you trust.

When you speak, either in private with God or in a conversation with a Christian, Jesus Christ will answer. Even before the runaway son got home to his father, the father saw his son in the distance and ran to him. In fact, God in Jesus Christ is already running toward you. As Jesus Christ said, "Listen! I am standing at the door, knocking; if you hear my voice and open the door, I will come in to you and eat with you and you with me" (Revelation 3:20).

Nicodemus said to Jesus, "How is it possible to be born from above? I am who I am. I cannot be different from who I am already. I cannot start all over again, can I?" Jesus replied, "Simply trust me. You will become someone new. Your new life will be a gift from God" (see John 3:1-21 author's paraphrase). This new life, abundant and everlasting, is Jesus Christ's gift to everyone who follows him.

Meeting Jesus Christ requires making room for him in your life and claiming him as your Guide and Shepherd along the way. Jesus Christ always comes to you. The appropriate response at each moment is to go to him. Despite your doubts, your fears, your denials, you simply have to say "Yes" to Jesus Christ. This new relationship depends on your listening, repenting, and trusting and on being empowered by Jesus Christ. As Jesus told his disciples, "I do not call you servants... but I have called you friends" (John 15:15).

When you speak and listen, your decision is one major step in your journey. There are many more way stations through which you must pass. You will still fail many times. Many questions will remain. You will still have doubts. But on your journey you now have a guide: Jesus Christ. And as you follow Jesus Christ, he will shape your mind, touch your heart, and guide your feet. The best is yet to come.

Eight

CAN I START AGAIN?

The salvation Jesus offered included, but went beyond spiritual well-being. Because Jesus loved the whole person, his goal was to help each person become whole.

James K. Wagner

At dawn [Jesus] appeared again in the temple courts, where all the people gathered around him, and he sat down to teach them. The teachers of the law and the Pharisees brought in a woman caught in adultery. They made her stand before the group and said to Jesus, "Teacher, this woman was caught in the act of adultery. In the Law Moses commanded us to stone such women. Now what do you say?" They were using this question as a trap, in order to have a basis for accusing him.

But Jesus bent down and started to write on the ground with his finger. When they kept on questioning him, he straightened up and said to them, "If any one of you is without sin, let him be the first to throw a stone at her." Again he stooped down and wrote on the ground.

At this, those who heard began to go away one at a time, the older ones first, until only Jesus was left, with the woman still standing there. Jesus straightened up and asked her, "Woman, where are they? Has no one condemned you?"

"No one, sir," she said.

"Then neither do I condemn you," Jesus declared. "Go now and leave your life of sin."

(John 8:2-11 NIV)

A large crowd followed and pressed around [Jesus]. And a woman was there who had been subject to bleeding for twelve years. She had suffered a great deal under the care of many doctors and had spent all she had, yet instead of getting better she grew worse. When she heard about Jesus, she came up behind him in the crowd and touched his cloak, because she thought, "If I just touch his clothes, I will be healed." Immediately her bleeding stopped and she felt in her body that she was freed from her suffering. (Mark 5:24-29 NIV)

Why did crowds of people constantly gather to get near Jesus? The simplest answer is that they were drawn to Jesus' power over failures and sickness. A woman caught in adultery was forgiven and could begin her life anew. A woman sick for years felt her suffering flow out of her body. Jesus forgave people and healed people—everyone wanted to feel his touch. As the New Testament describes Jesus' ministry, "As the sun was setting, all those who had any who were sick with various kinds of diseases brought them to [Jesus]; and he laid his hands on each of them and cured them" (Luke 4:40). Today, people still come to feel Jesus Christ's healing power over our failures; our brokenness; our illnesses of body, mind, and spirit.

BLESSINGS OF FORGIVENESS AND WHOLENESS

"Grace strikes us when we are in great pain and restlessness. It strikes us when we walk through the dark valley of a meaningless and empty life. It seeks us when we feel that our separation is deeper than usual." Paul Tillich

Jesus Christ offers people who enter into a relationship and journey with him two particular blessings: forgiveness and wholeness. Salvation as a complete relationship with Jesus Christ is not just a journey that leads to feeling close to God; salvation also means being "forgiven" and "made whole." When we speak about salvation, we mean that Jesus Christ intends that everyone have a healthy body, sound mind, and joyful spirit and that everyone be reconciled with God and be in harmony with other people. Such an abundant life is a gift from God through Jesus Christ.

All of us have broken places in our lives. Some of us live within destructive relationships in our families and at work. Some of us are victims of abuse, or we abuse others. Some of us are addicted to a variety of crutches: alcohol or other drugs, pornography, gambling, or compulsive behaviors. Some of us are bound by desires for power and prestige. Some of us are hiding secrets that we cannot name out loud. Some of us are blind and deaf to the needs of the people around us. Some of us are fatally ill. In our spiritual journey along the way, is there forgiveness and wholeness for people like us? Can we be refreshed and renewed in our journey?

Writer Anne Lamott tells her own contemporary story in *Traveling Mercies* of finding refreshment and renewal by Jesus Christ. Her own life included addictions and disastrous relationships, but then Jesus Christ entered her story. "I thought about my life and my brilliant hilarious progressive friends, I thought about what everyone would think of me if I became a Christian, and it seemed an utterly impossible thing that simply could not be allowed to happen….And one week later when I went back to church…I felt like—*something* was rocking me in its bosom, holding me like a scared kid, and I opened up to that feeling—and it washed over me."

In Jesus Christ, God offers us a relationship that does not tear down but builds up, does not condemn but forgives, does not wound but heals. God's saving, forgiving, and healing power is given without strings attached.

FORGIVENESS

The word *forgive* is from the old English, meaning that someone "gives something for" another person. We find the clearest sign of Jesus' power to forgive in his relationship with his friend Peter.

On the night of Jesus' arrest and trial, Jesus' closest friend for three years, Peter, was asked three times if he knew Jesus. As Jesus was being interrogated and beaten in the house next to him, Peter was given the opportunity to stand up and speak out on behalf of Jesus. Three times Peter denied even knowing Jesus. In Jesus' darkest hour, his best friend deserted him. But then, as Jesus hung on the cross, he said about the people who killed him and about his friends who deserted him, "Father, forgive them; for they do not know what they are doing" (Luke 23:34).

After the crucifixion and death of Jesus, Peter knew that he had failed Jesus and in shame went into hiding with the other disciples. Jesus came to them and showed them his wounds. In spite of his suffering, Jesus offered both peace and the power to forgive. In this offering of peace it was clear that Jesus not only forgave but empowered Peter and the other disciples (John 20). If Jesus could forgive Peter, Jesus can also forgive us.

> *"Without being forgiven, released from the consequences of what we have done—we would remain the victims of its consequences forever, not unlike the sorcerer's apprentice who lacked the magic formula to break the spell."*
>
> *Doris Donnelly*

Forgiveness is an eternal quality of God. An Old Testament song proclaims God's forgiving power:

Bless the LORD...who forgives all your iniquity,
    who heals all your diseases,
who redeems your life from the Pit,
    who crowns you with steadfast love and mercy....
As far as the east is from the west,
    so far [God] removes our transgressions from us.
As a father has compassion for his children,
    so the Lord has compassion for those who fear him.
                    (Psalm 103:1-4, 12-13)

Forgiveness is not just a nice idea or a few simple words; forgiveness is a visible action. Jesus preached forgiveness, but he also practiced forgiveness. To unfaithful Peter and to the adulterous woman, Jesus acknowledged the power of their failures, spoke about disordered relationships, and then offered restoration that made them whole. Every time Jesus offered forgiveness, lives were changed.

In each case, Jesus Christ initiates forgiveness. His forgiveness is more than "Kiss and make up," "Shake hands together," or "Can't we all just get along together?" Even before people know that they need to be forgiven, Jesus Christ acts. When Jesus Christ acts, he takes away the captivating power of our wrong ways and cancels the debts our failures have created. Change happens. There is a purifying freedom that releases us from bonds that have held us back.

At its heart forgiveness means being brought back into a right relationship with God that frees us. As the father forgave his runaway son, so God can also forgive people like us who have run in many strange ways. As Jesus forgave the adulterous woman while other people wanted to stone her, so Jesus Christ can reconcile us to himself and to God.

Once we have been forgiven, it is necessary for us to forgive other people. As Jesus taught his followers to pray, which we will discuss more in the next chapter, Jesus suggested that we ask of God, "Forgive us our sins, for we ourselves forgive everyone indebted to us" (Luke 11:4). In one translation of Jesus' words, Jesus asked his followers to pray, "Loose the cords of mistakes binding us, as we release the strands we hold of others" or "Forgive our hidden past, the secret shames, as we consistently forgive what others hide" (Syrian Aramaic version of Luke 11:4).

Forgiving another person is hard. Only when we recognize that Jesus Christ has forgiven us and that we have received divine mercy can we then forgive and offer mercy to someone else. To err is to be human. We can forgive other people only when we recognize that we are just like them. Forgiving other people is risky, costly, and uncertain. Forgiveness is not excusing an unjust behavior or action. Forgiveness does not necessarily include forgetting; the past remains with us. But forgiveness is how Christians live and act as we face the future.

In the middle of the last century, the German Nazis attempted to exterminate all the Jews in Europe, along with many other "lesser humans," such as gypsies, homosexuals, and the small number of Christians who protested the Nazi program of holocaust. Among those Christians persecuted was a Dutch woman named Corrie ten Boom. In one concentration camp where she and her sister were held, her sister died under the persecution. After the liberation, Corrie ten Boom often preached about her experience. After one of her sermons, a former prison guard from her concentration camp greeted her. She struggled and prayed as he put out his hand to shake hers. "I tried to smile. I struggled to raise my hand. I could not. And so again I breathed a silent prayer. . . . As I took his hand a most incredible thing happened. From my shoulder along my arm and through my hand a current seemed to pass from me to him, while into my heart sprang a love for this stranger that almost overwhelmed me. And so I discovered that it is not on our forgiveness any more than on our goodness that the world's healing hinges, but on God's. When Jesus tells us to love our enemies, he gives, along with the command, the love itself."

Jesus gave us some particular examples of how to forgive. He told us that when what is ours is taken, we are not to demand the stolen object back. We are to bless people who curse us and pray for people who mistreat us (Luke 6:27-28, 29-30). Jesus told his friend Peter to forgive his brother seventy-seven times (Matthew 18:21-22). Following Jesus' example, forgiveness means releasing another person from our own judgment, guilt, and punishment.

When President Gerald Ford pardoned former president Richard Nixon after the Watergate scandal, Ford offered the pardon on a Sunday afternoon after worshiping and receiving Holy Communion at an Episcopal congregation in Washington, DC. Nixon had not asked for a pardon and at first even refused to accept it. But as Ford wrote at the time, "I...will receive justice without mercy if I fail to show mercy." Following Ford's action, a *Time* magazine essay stated, "Each of us is to a degree lost, tied to the rest of humanity—and to God—by fragile strands of grace, strands that fray and break. Pardon is a favor that we may sometimes be in a position to grant, but more important, it is one that we will always need."

When we walk with Jesus Christ, we understand that when we lose our way, when we journey down some wrong paths, or even when we lead other people astray, our failures are not held against us. Nor can we hold the failures of other people against them.

WHOLENESS

"Are any among you sick? They should call for the elders of the church and have them pray over them.... The prayer of faith will save the sick." (James 5:14-15)

Just as God in Jesus Christ forgives us, through the Holy Spirit, God offers wholeness in every aspect of our lives. Illustrations of God's healing power are all around us. For example, a great number of scientific studies have indicated that people of faith have more healthy lives than people without faith. Christians agree. We believe that through Jesus Christ, God works to restore our minds, souls, bodies, and relationships.

Christians, as well as everyone everywhere, struggle with physical illnesses, mental crises, dark nights of the soul, and breakdowns in every kind of relationship. Just think about people in your own family. How many members of your family have physical problems, mental difficulties, spiritual crises, and broken relationships? The number is overwhelming and encompasses all persons everywhere.

Increasingly, we look to modern, high-tech medicine to heal all that ails us. Professional healers can cure acute infections, repair damaged hearts, or replace a kidney. Trained counselors can often help put individual lives and relationships back in order. Many people can testify about the power of medical and psychological miracles. Often, professional healers are successful in their efforts, and Christians must take advantage of every medical and psychological resource available.

Our medical and psychological professionals cannot do everything, however. Whenever we get sick, we want a magic pill to make us well. When we face crises, we want a counseling session to make everyone feel good. When we get serious, however, we know that there is no magic pill. Psychologists cannot fix every dysfunctional life or relationship. We all have seen situations when a person looks up to a doctor and says, "Doctor, help me." The doctor then replies, "I'm sorry. There's nothing I can do." People still get sick and die. Many acute and chronic illnesses—high blood pressure, heart disease, arthritis, AIDS, and cancer—and psychological disorders—depression, abusive lifestyles, obsessive compulsive disorder, anxiety, and stress—still destroy lives.

Christians believe that there is more to healthy lives than good blood-cell counts and stable EKGs. There is more to healing than pills and scalpels. There is more to whole relationships than a one-hour discussion with a therapist. Those of us who follow Jesus Christ know that there is another power to heal. Christians have always known that through Jesus Christ, God can comfort and strengthen us and restore brokenness.

QUESTIONS ABOUT WHOLENESS

Does God care when we hurt and are broken? We believe that God does care. Prayers for wholeness are an essential part of the Christian life. Like a child asking a parent for help, we speak to Jesus Christ when we hurt and ask God to kiss away our pain. We speak, knowing that God is listening.

If wholeness does not happen, does it mean that we did not have enough faith? No. Wholeness depends not upon what we do but upon what God in Christ through the Holy Spirit wants to do with us. The good news is that God, especially God in Christ, wants us to be well and whole. To pray for wholeness, for ourselves or for others, is simply one part of what it means for us to trust God and to follow Jesus Christ.

What is our role in wholeness? We have to be responsible people. We have our own part to play—eat right, exercise, be involved with other people, care for other persons, get medical care, and go for counseling. God will not unilaterally undo the injury we do to our own bodies and minds and relationships. Sometimes we must claim responsibility for our own pain. Sometimes we must honestly acknowledge that we cause our own problems. Often we are sick because we have put ourselves in the wrong place and have done the wrong thing. On these occasions, we cannot be healed until we step away from the forbidden place. But when we do our part, God then works with us and adds to our efforts.

Is the wholeness God provides magic? No one can simply touch us and make us well; no one alive is just like Jesus Christ. Certain preachers we may see on television, despite their claims, may not be absolutely truthful. Every follower of Jesus Christ, however, can be a channel of God's love. Followers of Jesus Christ remind one another that God desires that everyone be whole and well, and they pray accordingly.

Will we be spared suffering? Many of us are in mental and physical pain. There is no divine promise of immediate cure or instant relief from suffering. But God is beside us in our pain, sickness, injury, and estrangement from one another. Jesus suffered on the cross. Nevertheless, God was there. Especially when we are hurting, Jesus Christ is beside us.

"Christianity doesn't in any way lessen suffering. What it does is enable you to take it, to face it, to work through it and eventually to convert it." Terry Waite

Reynolds Price, poet, author, and professor at Duke University, was diagnosed with a tumor on his spinal cord that left him in constant pain, paralyzed below his waist, and confined to a wheelchair. As he wrote in his book about this ordeal, "I asked a thousand times for healing, for ease and a longer life. But calamities continued, and even the repetition of 'Your will be done' had come to sound empty." In the end, however, Price's relationship with Jesus Christ intensified and led him to pray "for life as long as I have work to do, and work as long as I have life"; and his life was more "rewarding and productive" after his prayers. Price knew that Jesus was with him throughout his journey, even when it did not include curing him.

Healing toward wholeness is more a process than a possession. Healing is what happens to us in our journey along the way rather than our final destination. But there is the promise of a world in which God will "wipe every tear....Death will be no more; mourning and crying and pain will be no more" (Revelation 21:4).

HOW TO BE FORGIVEN AND MADE WHOLE

"To say that 'Jesus saves' is to say that when we have strayed from our true home in God, when our souls are sick and at loose ends, he brings us back and heals and unifies us for strong and victorious living."

Georgia Harkness

The good news is that Jesus Christ desires that each person receive the reconciling, forgiving, loving, and restoring power of God. Jesus Christ yearns to transform our brokenness into wholeness.

So how do we ask God for forgiveness and healing? There are a few common steps toward the way of forgiveness and wholeness:

1. Relax in the presence of God. Be quiet and trust in God (Psalm 46:10). Because Jesus Christ is always with us, stop talking; turn off the television, radio, and computer. Then take a few short, deep breaths and listen for the voice of God.

2. Name your pain. Tell specifically and accurately what you need (Matthew 20:32). Admit your failures. Tell what you have done wrong. Speak about your brokenness. Do not add ifs, ands, and buts; state clearly where you need God's presence.

3. Relinquish control. Trust that God is listening (Psalm 4:5). Do not tell God how to act, but ask God to set aside your doubts and fears. Yield to God. Listen, and feel God's touch.

4. Participate in the forgiveness and wholeness. Pray hard, and do your part. As Jesus said to the adulterous woman, "Go your way, and from now on do not sin again" (John 8:11). If you have broken a law, do not do it again. Stop doing what you have done wrong; then make restitution. If you have lied, tell the truth. If you have broken something, fix it. If you are damaging your body, stop it. If you need to see a doctor, make an appointment. If you have offended someone, apologize. Forgiveness and wholeness require more than just words; they also require action.

5. Anticipate results. God invites us to receive the gift, but we must accept the gift for it to work (Romans 5:1-2). You can be forgiven and made whole. When wholeness happens, say "Thank you, Jesus Christ."

WALKING FORWARD

God wants you to be whole. Jesus Christ's vision for you is that you will be forgiven, physical healing will be strengthened, mental and emotional balance will be achieved, spiritual health will be enhanced, and relationships will be restored. These are gifts from God, who searches for you and invites you in the walk.

Nine

How Do I Speak to God?

My secret is very simple: I pray. Through prayer I become one in love with Christ.

Mother Teresa

One day Jesus was praying in a certain place. When he finished, one of his disciples said to him, "Lord, teach us to pray...."

[Jesus] said to them, "When you pray, say:

'Father,
hallowed be your name,
your kingdom come.
Give us each day our daily bread.
Forgive us our sins,
    for we also forgive everyone who sins
        against us.
And lead us not into temptation.'"

Then [Jesus] said to them, "Suppose one of you has a friend, and he goes to him at midnight and says, 'Friend, lend me three loaves of bread, because a friend of mine on a journey has come to me, and I have nothing to set before him.'

"Then the one inside answers, 'Don't bother me. The door is already locked.…I can't get up and give you anything.' I tell you, though he will not get up and give him the bread because he is his friend, yet because of the man's boldness he will get up and give him as much as he needs.

"So I say to you: Ask and it will be given to you; seek and you will find; knock and the door will be opened to you.…

"Which of you fathers, if your son asks for a fish, will give him a snake instead? Or if he asks for an egg, will give him a scorpion? If you then, though you are evil, know how to give good gifts to your children, how much more will your Father in heaven give the Holy Spirit to those who ask him!" (Luke 11:1-13 NIV)

In the classic 1967 movie *Cool Hand Luke*, Luke, a prisoner, escapes from a southern prison camp and chain gang and finds refuge in an empty church. Luke begins to question God: Where am I supposed to fit in? What have you got in mind for me? What am I to do now?

Jesus' friends were in the same place as Cool Hand Luke. Like Jesus himself, Jesus' twelve closest friends had all left behind their occupations and families. Tax collectors, fishermen, and political activists were now traveling companions with this radical teacher who was increasingly upsetting the establishment. These followers had no steady income and no home to return to each evening. Their childhood friends were long gone. What they recognized, however, was that in the midst of all this turmoil, Jesus remained calm and focused. While strong winds blew, Jesus stayed strong. What was his secret?

The disciples suspected that Jesus' strength came from the time he spent with God in prayer. Jesus was a man of prayer. He prayed morning, noon, and night. He prayed when alone by himself; he prayed with other people; he prayed in public; he prayed in the Temple in Jerusalem; and he prayed even while on the cross. They needed some of that strength. So Jesus taught his friends how to speak with God; he provided them with the directions to the map in which God is at the center.

When you get into trouble, whom are you going to call? When you face major decisions, who gives you advice? When you lose your job, who lends you a sympathetic ear? When you receive three job offers, who offers counsel? When you wake up in the middle of the night sweating about an unresolved problem, who listens to you? When you are at a crossroad, who points you in the right direction?

WHAT IS PRAYER?

"Prayer is none other than an expanding of our hearts in the presence of God."

John Calvin

Christians through prayer call on God at all these times. For Christians, prayer is a way of living every moment of every day with the possibility of being in instant communication with God. Better than a wireless communication network or a global positioning system, God is always accessible to people who pray for guidance in the journey. The word prayer comes from a word that means "to petition" or "to beg." Prayer is a person sharing with God the most needful parts of her or his life, begging for assistance and guidance, and then listening to

God's answer. Through prayer we have an immediate, one-on-one communication with God; no pen and paper, no phones, no digital transmissions, no other person, and no e-mail addresses are required. The more time we spend with God in prayer, the more we know about God, the more we know about ourselves, and the more wisdom we have about the next fork in the road. In prayer, we surrender ourselves to God, believing that God will treat us well and guide us faithfully.

"Whisper in my heart, and tell me you are there."
Augustine

Almost everyone prays; it is a basic human instinct to talk with the God who created us. Some people, however, pray only in times of crisis, and even then they are not sure anyone is listening. These people pray only when in desperate need of help: a mother in labor, a child taking a test, a person having second thoughts about his or her upcoming marriage, an employee just before a downsizing of a company, a person on a crashing plane, or a nation in times of disaster. All these crises are good times to pray. Good times to pray also include watching the birth of a child, passing a test, beginning a marriage, getting a new job, surviving a life-threatening event, or in days when one's country is blessed.

Prayers may sometimes lead people astray. The old English children's prayer "Now I lay me down to sleep, I pray the Lord my soul to keep. If I should die before I wake, I pray the Lord my soul to take" seems to point in a wrong direction. To tell children that they may die in their sleep may simply encourage them to sleep in their parents' bed. A better nighttime prayer for children may be this one: "God in heaven, hear my prayer, keep me in thy loving care. Be my guide in all I do, and bless all those who love me too." Prayers can also reveal our worst instincts: "God bless me, my wife, and my two kids, us four and no more. Amen." Most prayers are better than this.

"You can't pray a lie."　　　　　　　*Mark Twain*

Prayer is an intimate, private, personal conversation with God, through Jesus Christ, empowered by the Holy Spirit. Through prayer we grow in our relationship with God and receive the guidance we need in our spiritual journeys. Think about prayer in this way. If you meet someone whom you would like to know better, you engage in a conversation. After a brief conversation, if you connected with each other, you plan to get together again and continue the conversation. The more you talk with the other person, the stronger the relationship grows. The longer the conversations, the more you know about the other person, the more the other person knows about you, and the more you support each other's way through life. When you have formed this kind of friendship through intimate, deep conversation, even if you do not talk with your friend for days or even years, when you get back together, you simply pick up the friendship and conversation where you left off. Christians strive to form this same kind of intimate relationship with God through prayer.

HOW TO PRAY: BASIC QUESTIONS

A mother we know taught her son while he was still a young child to pray each night before bedtime. Together they prayed for "glads, sads, and sorries." "Glads" were celebrations throughout the day; "sads" named disappointments; and "sorries" offered apologies for wrong actions and thoughts. What a wonderful way to begin to pray!

Who can pray? We believe that everyone can pray! A distinctive belief of Protestant Christians is summarized in the words "the priesthood of all believers." This means that everyone can be in immediate communication with God. Paid church professionals do not have superior access to God; every one of us can speak directly with God. The priesthood of all believers also means that every Christian has an obligation to pray for other people, for crisis situations, and for everything in creation. In other words, everyone can have a conversation with God that is a local call, not needing an operator or requiring a roaming surcharge.

Rick Moody once wrote in an essay entitled "Why I Pray," "I consider myself a good example of this democratic aspect of prayer. I use the more-than-occasional four-letter oath. I am not opposed to sexually explicit renderings in film or literature. I have a tattoo. I favor same-sex marriage. I have made a lot of mistakes and I expect to continue doing so. Yet, most mornings, and sometimes on the subway or in cars or on airplanes or in the silence before a movie starts, I engage in this dialogue in which I ask to stay alive and not to do anything dramatically stupid in the next twenty-four hours."

When do we pray? The New Testament instructs us to pray constantly (1 Thessalonians 5:17). But no one can pray every moment of every day; it is physically impossible. Yet, there are many occasions every day when prayer is appropriate: in the morning when you awake, when you hear on the radio about an international disaster, when a friend describes a crisis in her or his life, when an important decision must be made, before a meal, with a child before bed, and at night before you go to sleep. Throughout our lives we pray when a child is born, on the first day of school, at a graduation, when we meet the perfect person, when we change jobs, and when a parent dies. Every time is a good time to pray.

How should we pray? Find a quiet place where you will not be interrupted for at least five minutes. Your special place could be your back porch, in your car with the radio turned off, or in your office with the phone off the hook. Sit comfortably, or you may stand or kneel. Do not hurry. Listen to your heart, and slow down your breathing. Try this simple exercise: Breathe in, hold the air in your lungs for five seconds, then breathe out. Repeat this breathing exercise five times in a row. Your breathing, your heart rate, and your mind will slow down and relax. You have now begun to pray.

THE LORD'S PRAYER

What should we pray? There are excellent models of prayer throughout the Bible. One primary model is the prayer Jesus taught his friends (which is at the beginning of this chapter). We call it "The Lord's Prayer." This prayer (one version in Luke; one version in Matthew) has been used by practically every Christian since Jesus taught it to his friends. This short prayer is used in public worship, in funerals, in weddings, and in private devotions. One excellent way of praying is to memorize The Lord's Prayer and say it slowly, phrase by phrase, once a day. The following translation (there are hundreds of different translations) is one that many Christians use:

Our Father in heaven, hallowed be your name.
Your kingdom come.
   Your will be done, on earth as in heaven.
Give us today our daily bread.
Forgive us our sins
   as we forgive those who sin against us.
Save us from the time of trial, and deliver us from evil.
For the kingdom, the power, and the glory are yours,
now and for ever. Amen.

The Lord's Prayer has six major movements or principles: praise to God, a hope for the world, a call for assistance, a plea for forgiveness, a request for protection, and a final affirmation. These six guiding principles may be the foundation of a Christian's prayer life.

The first two sections of Jesus' prayer focus on God and God's plan for the world.

1. "Our Father in heaven, hallowed be your name." The best word to describe this opening is "Awesome!" Jesus declares that God rules over the entire universe. This God-centered prayer reminds us that God is God and that we people are not gods. When we offer these words, Christians can also add to this affirmation of praise by thanking God for blessings such as life, health, family, job, and friends.

We do not believe that by calling God "Father," Jesus intended to say that God is a male. God created both women and men in God's own image (Genesis 1:27). Rather, Jesus used both the name and metaphor of "Father" to declare that God is the One who created the universe and still rules over everything. "Father" means a Parent-God who loves, protects, guides, corrects, and nurtures us even better than any good parent should. If, for you, the image of God as "father" carries negative connotations, open your prayer with another biblical image for God—light, mother, dove, protector, lover, provider, shepherd, or helper—that conveys God's encompassing presence.

2. "Your kingdom come. Your will be done, on earth as in heaven." Jesus' prayer puts God first, seeking God's wise authority over everything—or in other words, "God, make things right!" With these words, we ask God to create good people, a nation that is just, and a peaceful world. In other words, "Help us let go of our anxieties and trust your [God's] presence." This sentence is Jesus' clearest promise that God will give each of us the guidance we need in our walk along the way. When we pray these words of petition for the world, we may also add where and how we are going to help bring in God's kingdom by sharing our material resources and by volunteering our time for a worthy cause.

"The point of prayer is not to tell God what we want, but to receive what we need. It is not approaching God with our demands, but listening for God's leading. It is not seeking our will, but learning to discern God's will. This is so important to understand in a culture that caters to our every whim. Prayer isn't about me—it is about God."
James Mulholland

The next three movements of The Lord's Prayer give specifics to our requests for God's guidance in our lives:

3. "Give us today our daily bread." "Help me" is the next part of the prayer. Jesus asks God to provide not whatever we want but whatever we need. There is no need that we have, whether food, health, success, friendship, or love, that we cannot ask of God. We must be careful, however, to distinguish between what we truly need and what we just desire. When we pray for assistance, we tell God what we need to make it through the day and are assured that God will faithfully supply our needs. Likewise, we must be careful not to become too self-centered about our requests. In a world full of hungry people, our prayers and actions must also be directed toward everyone having enough to eat. When we pray for ourselves, we must intentionally also commend to God the needs of the poor, the hungry, the war-ravaged, and the sick and commit ourselves to serve them all.

4. "Forgive us our sins as we forgive those who sin against us." "Pardon me" begins this fourth part of the prayer. We ask for forgiveness when we wrong ourselves, other people, and God. When we abuse ourselves; when we hurt another person by anything we say, do, or think; and when we offend God by our thoughts and deeds, this prayer asks God to cleanse us. The prayer also indicates that we need to forgive other people. Forgiveness is not just something God does; we must also forgive others when they hurt us by what they say, do, or think. At the very same time when we ask for forgiveness for ourselves, we also confess how we have failed God and other people, knowing that God will forgive whatever we have done and give us the power to forgive others.

5. "Save us from the time of trial, and deliver us from evil." "Protect me" is also included in the prayer. Jesus encourages us to pray to overcome every difficulty and temptation throughout our journey of life. Our biggest temptation is to put ourselves at the top of our list of priorities. For example, in our affluent North American culture, we have a tendency to be seduced by money, career, power, and privilege. We are tempted to believe that "success" in the financial, professional, and personal areas of our lives is the key to the good life. This prayer acknowledges that it is only with God's help that we can put God first. As we pray for protection, we ask God to shelter us from evil inclinations and tempting situations.

6. The last few words of The Lord's Prayer—**"For the kingdom, the power, and the glory are yours, now and for ever. Amen"**—were added by the early followers of Jesus. These words remind us that God is the ultimate power; and the final word, "Amen," acts as an affirmation of every word of the prayer. In other words, when we say "Amen," we say that all the above words are our vow to God. This prayer is not just a collection of words but points us to how we might live.

In summary, Jesus taught everyone who follows him how to pray. Try starting with this prayer:

Awesome God.
Make things right.
Help me.
Pardon me.
Protect me.
Amen.

OTHER WAYS TO PRAY

There are also many other ways to pray. We may pray by simply focusing on one thing: a word of thanks, an acknowledgment of failure, a personal request for ourselves or someone else, or a concern. When we receive a blessing, we give thanks. When we fail, we tell God we are sorry. While driving a car, we commend a friend to God. When we hear about a tragedy on television, we ask God to care for the people involved. When facing a major decision, we ask for wisdom. The best prayer is the prayer that comes from your heart. About what are you excited? Tell Jesus Christ. About what are you anxious? Mention it to Jesus Christ. How are you hurting? Ask God for help. What is giving you joy? Say, "Thank you, Jesus Christ." All of these prayers work not because of what we say but because God is our loving Parent.

The Bible also contains other ways we might pray. For example, the book of Psalms, the songbook of the Bible, teaches us other excellent ways to pray. These 150 songs express the whole range of human emotions, from rage to joy to agony to revenge.

Look at just one prayer song: Psalm 23. Tradition tells us that David, the boy who defeated the giant Goliath and who was a future king of Israel, wrote Psalm 23 while fleeing for his life from the current king, Saul, who was trying to kill him. The following is the traditional translation of this prayer:

The LORD is my shepherd; I shall not want.
He maketh me to lie down in green pastures:
    he leadeth me beside the still waters.
He restoreth my soul: he leadeth me
    in the paths of righteousness for his name's sake.
Yea, though I walk
        through the valley of the shadow of death,
    I will fear no evil:
for thou art with me;
    thy rod and thy staff they comfort me.

Thou preparest a table before me
    in the presence of mine enemies;
thou anointest my head with oil;
    my cup runneth over.
Surely goodness and mercy shall follow me
    all the days of my life:
and I will dwell in the house of the Lord for ever.

                         (Psalm 23 KJV)

For many people, simply saying or singing this biblical song is a deep prayer for comfort. This prayer is often used at funerals, when people look to God for strength and courage and the assurance of life beyond death. The Bible is full of prayers like Psalm 23 that you can use that speak directly to the needs in your everyday life.

DOES PRAYER WORK?

"To pray for others means to offer others a hospitable place where I can really listen to their needs and pains."
Henri J. M. Nouwen

Did Jesus give good advice to his friends? Did his prayer offer them the peace they were seeking? We know that whether we pray The Lord's Prayer, Psalm 23, our own private prayers, or prayers with other people, the results of prayer are not always certain. That is, prayer is not magic. Prayer is not like an Aladdin's lamp that, when rubbed as the magic words are spoken, will produce a genie to grant our wishes.

All of us who have prayed for something have felt at times that our prayers were unanswered. Sometimes the fault is our own; we have asked for the wrong thing. If a child asks Santa Claus for a bike and a pony and a swimming pool and a new brother, the requests may not be fully granted. The answer to your prayers may be "Yes" or "No" or "Not now" or simply silence. Sometimes we are so busy talking in prayer that we forget to listen. We need to listen as well as speak, to hear as well as be heard.

Prayer brings us into close communion with God. The conversion in 1907 of an English woman named Evelyn Underhill came during a period of deep, mystical searching and prayer, after which she became a leading teacher about prayer and the contemplative life: "One day when I was praying, quite suddenly a Voice seemed to speak to me—with tremendous staccato sharpness and clearness. It only said one short thing, first in Latin and then in English! Please don't think I am going in for psychic automatisms or horrors of that sort. It has never happened again, and I don't want it to. Of course I know all about the psychological aspect and am not *hallucinated*. All the same, I simply cannot believe that there was not something deeper, more real, not me at all, behind. The effect was terrific. Sort of nailed me to the floor for half an hour, which went as a flash. I felt definitely called out and settled, once for all—that any falling back or leaving off, after that, will be an unpardonable treason. That sense has persisted—it marked a sort of turning point and the end of all the remorse and worry, and banging about."

Prayer often demands much of us. When we pray, we cannot put all the burden on God to fulfill our prayers. An old Russian proverb reminds us, "Pray to God, but continue to row to the shore." Sometimes the answer we receive to our prayers demands that we behave differently and live in a new way. When we pray, we have to be alert that our life may change in ways we never expected. An old story makes this point. During a great flood, a man is stranded on the roof of his house. The man prays to God for help. All of a sudden, a boat comes along and the people on board offer assistance; but the man turns the boaters away. Next, a helicopter comes and the crew members offer to lift him to safety; but again the man refuses. The man again prays, "God, save me." God replies, "You've already turned away two of my offers. How many more do you want?"

What is the value of prayer, therefore, if we are not always certain of the results and if we may have to do lots of the work? Prayer brings joy (John 16:24); peace (Philippians 4:7); and, most of all, a stronger relationship with Jesus Christ. The greatest gift we receive in prayer is the gift of the presence of God; we know that we are not alone wherever we are along the way. A few people describe their experience in prayer as being covered with warm oil or filled with a warm spirit or even being hit by a bolt of lightning. Others of us never have such experiences. But by simply having a close, intimate conversation with God, we learn more about Jesus Christ and more about ourselves. What happens in prayer is not that we necessarily hear an actual voice giving us something specific to do, although this may happen. Prayer is most effective when it helps us discern Jesus Christ's presence in our lives. It changes our own personal perspective into God's perspective, and it becomes clearer which road we are to follow.

Jesus told us that even if we do not see and hear God in our prayers, God is with us. Jesus said, "Ask, and it will be given you; search, and you will find; knock, and the door will be opened for you. For everyone who asks receives, and everyone who searches finds, and for everyone who knocks, the door will be opened" (Matthew 7:7-8). Jesus then provided an example to prove we can trust God when we pray: "Is there anyone among you who, if your child asks for bread, will give a stone? Or if the child asks for a fish, will give a snake?" (Matthew 7:9-10). Just as we human beings are attentive and giving to our children and would never give them anything that would harm them, likewise Jesus declared that God is even more attentive and giving: "If you then ... know how to give good gifts to your children, how much more will your Father in heaven give good things to those who ask him!" (Matthew 7:11).

ABOVE ALL, PRAY!

As you continue your journey along the way, above all, pray. There are many forks in the road, and at every crossroad we need the guidance that prayer may provide. Mohandas Gandhi, the nonviolent liberator of modern India, declared that "prayer is not an old woman's idle amusement. Properly understood and applied, prayer is the most potent instrument of action." God wants to be with you 24/7/365. God has given you the tools. Pray.

Ten

HOW CAN I MAKE A LIFE AND NOT JUST A LIVING?

Lord Jesus, you be the needle and I will be the cotton thread. You go through first and I will follow wherever you may lead.   *Prayer from Zaire*

A certain ruler asked [Jesus], "Good teacher, what must I do to inherit eternal life?"

"Why do you call me good?" Jesus answered. "No one is good—except God alone. You know the commandments: 'Do not commit adultery, do not murder, do not steal, do not give false testimony, honor your father and mother.'"

"All these I have kept since I was a boy," [the ruler] said.

When Jesus heard this, he said to him, "You still lack one thing. Sell everything you have and give to the poor, and you will have treasure in heaven. Then come, follow me."

When he heard this, [the ruler] became very sad, because he was a man of great wealth.

(Luke 18:18-23 NIV)

What is the source of a good life? The mantra "Don't worry. Be happy" since the 1960s has for many people been the definition of a good life. We live in a society where "the pursuit of happiness" is an inalienable right promised to us even by the United States Constitution. When asked about their dreams for their children, many parents declare that they hope most fervently that their children will be "happy." We seem to believe that if we have a good marriage, healthy children, prominent careers, strong bodies, and a secure 401K, our lives will be good. Like Garrison Keillor, we want to live in communities where "all the men are strong, all the women good looking, and all the children above average." Do we achieve a good life by being happy?

David G. Myers writes that as average Americans we have more material things than ever before. But, "we have less happiness, more depression, more fragile relationships, less communal commitment, less vocational security, more crime, and more demoralized children."

The difficulty is that a pursuit of happiness or possessions has caused many of us to miss a good life. Too many people have become aggressively self-interested. Serial monogamy replaces committed relationships. Whatever we have is never quite enough. We all need an additional ten percent of income. Our bodies are run down. We yearn for a fulfilling job. Our families are stressed out. After pursuing happiness and possessions, however, just like persons who play so hard on a vacation that they come back exhausted, too many people are simply lost on the way.

As a follower of Jesus Christ, what is the way to discover a good life? Being Christian does not mean just saying that Jesus Christ is our guide. Being a Christian means living a life permeated by Christian virtues and practices. One way to have a good life is simply to be good.

A lawyer, a man with a career who made a good living, came to Jesus and asked him how to live a moral life. The lawyer had in life what many of us desire: position, a future, and security. But such things were not enough. This lawyer wanted to know how to live a life with meaning. Jesus answered by quoting two verses from the Old Testament: love God and love your neighbor (Matthew 22:34-40). Christians begin to live a good life in our journey on the way by following Jesus Christ and following these two principles. We call Jesus' response "The Great Commandment."

Being good is not some singular action or series of behaviors we undertake; being good is the way we live with Jesus Christ throughout the whole of our lives. For example, in the first years of the church in the ancient Roman Empire, the people of the Way dramatically increased in numbers, not because they went knocking on everyone's door and passing out the sayings of Jesus, but because Christians lived good lives that other people wanted to imitate. These first followers of Jesus Christ were compassionate toward everyone, especially the poor, slaves, and outcasts. Rodney Stark sums up this way of good living for the first Christians in *The Rise of Christianity*: "Christianity…arose in response to the misery, chaos, fear, and brutality of life in the urban Greco-Roman world.… To cities filled with the homeless and impoverished, Christianity offered charity as well as hope. To cities filled with newcomers and strangers, Christianity offered an immediate basis for attachments. To cities filled with orphans and widows, Christianity provided a new and expanded sense of family. To cities torn by violent ethnic strife, Christianity offered a new basis for social solidarity.…And to cities faced with epidemics, fires, and earthquakes, Christianity offered effective nursing services."

So how do Christians become good? Dietrich Bonhoeffer, the German theologian and pastor, refused to support the German Nazis and paid with his life. Corrie ten Boom forgave the jailer who helped kill her sister. These Christians led good lives that each of them would describe as happy. Many different Christians have created a variety of ways of living a good life. Through the ages Christians have tried to be good by sharing all their property (Acts 2:44-47), fighting wild animals in a Roman coliseum, going to live alone in a desert, joining with a group of women or men in an isolated community dedicated to worship and work, or traveling to a far-off country to care for other people. Still other Christians have given up sexual intercourse, refrained from smoking, abstained from alcohol, forbidden dancing, and renounced cosmetics and jewelry. Remember the old saying, "Don't smoke, drink, or chew; and stay away from those that do." Most of these ways of living good lives are not options for us. Most of us will experience less dramatic ways of following Jesus Christ, but all of us can make a difference in our own homes and communities and even throughout society.

Christians believe that there are certain ways to move beyond making a good living in order to live a good life. The underlying way is to follow in the footsteps of Jesus. As we follow Jesus Christ, there are two particular perspectives that we must adopt: loving God and loving our neighbor. Let's explore these ways of finding a good life.

FOLLOWING JESUS

When Jesus Christ offers us an abundant relationship with him that will never end, the result is that we want to be more like Jesus. We want to act toward other people the same way Jesus Christ has acted toward us. Because Jesus was compassionate, loving, and merciful, we desire to perform acts of compassion, deeds of love, and works of mercy so that we become more like him. In essence, we want to be apprentices to Jesus. As Jesus said, "Whoever serves me must follow me" (John 12:26).

There has been a long history in the church of people following Christ by imitating Jesus. The very word *Christian* means "a little Christ." Paul suggests that you "let the same mind be in you that was in Christ Jesus" (Philippians 2:5). One contemporary illustration of this method is found in the letters WWJD, which stand for "What Would Jesus Do?" This way of following Jesus Christ suggests that before we make any decision, we ask ourselves, *How would Jesus make this decision?* For example, if someone strikes you on one cheek, Jesus told us and showed us by his example to turn the other cheek. Because Jesus told us and showed us how to feed the hungry, to give drink to the thirsty, to welcome the stranger, to clothe the naked, and to share with other people God's good news, Christians are expected to do all these good things (Matthew 25:31-46).

Consider the life of Mother Teresa. Agnes Bojaxhiu was born in 1910 to a prosperous Albanian couple. She was baptized in the Roman Catholic Church. By age twelve, during a time of financial hardship in her family, she was attracted to the church's activities with the poor. In the book *Mother Teresa*, author Anne Sebba writes that by the time Bojaxhiu was sixteen years old, a local priest had told her, "If the thought that God may be calling you to serve him and your neighbor makes you happy, then that may be the very best proof of the genuineness of your vocation. Joy that comes from the depths of your being is like a compass by which you can tell what direction your life should follow. That is the case even when the road you must take is a difficult one." When she was eighteen, Bojaxhiu yearned to serve Jesus Christ in India. When she was twenty-one, she took a new Christian name, Teresa, as she assumed vows of poverty, chastity, and obedience as a Roman Catholic nun. She began her ministry in India by teaching rich girls in Calcutta. Then, at age thirty-six, she heard God calling her to care for the destitute of that city. Teresa began her work with no assistants, no money, no home, and without strong support from her church. As she wrote, "I was sure it was God's Voice. I was certain that He was calling me. The message was clear. I must leave the convent to help the poor by living among them. This was a command, something to be done, something definite. I knew where I had to be." Teresa, who then became the head of her community of nuns, took the name Mother Teresa and lived and worked among the poorest people in India (and in the world). In 1979, in recognition of her work, she won the Nobel Peace Prize. At her death in 1997, representatives of all six major religions in India praised her ministry with the dying, with those with handicapping conditions, and with the forgotten.

Yet, there are several difficulties connected with only using Jesus as an example as Mother Teresa did. For example, Jesus did not face every difficulty we face. Jesus did not directly address issues such as abortion, premarital sex, nuclear disarmament, drug use, Internet ethics, AIDS, global poverty, or embryonic stem cell research. Sometimes the Bible simply does not give clear answers to all our issues. A larger problem with WWJD is that as much as we may try to imitate Jesus, we cannot be Jesus. Jesus did many things that we cannot do. God gave us Jesus precisely because we cannot do everything good.

While following WWJD is a good idea as a general rule, it does not give us all the guidance we need to live a good life. We each have our own journey and our own way of following Jesus Christ.

LOVE GOD

To follow Jesus Christ means that we fundamentally change how we orient our lives. Most of us live as if everything and everybody should point at us. Too often we place ourselves at the center of the universe and want everyone to revolve around us. The Christian perspective, however, is as revolutionary as Copernicus's heavenly discovery: The sun does not circle the earth; the earth circles the sun. Jesus tells us to put God and other people at the center of the universe and to let every aspect of our lives revolve around our Creator and our neighbor. As Jesus said, "Those people who seek to save their lives will lose them, and those people who seek to lose their lives will save them" (John 12:25; author's translation).

So how do we Christians love God? We begin by acknowledging that love is not a feeling, such as what is experienced by a man who sees a beautiful woman. Rather, love is a way of living, a way of doing, a way of acting—like the behavior of an older person who cares for a dying spouse. As Paul suggested, love is a series of actions that include patience, kindness, and steadfastness (1 Corinthians 13). After Jesus loved us even to the point of death, he told us that we must love everyone in just the same way. In the Christian life, we cannot separate our faith from our daily life and our relationships. We have to talk the talk and walk the walk.

There are a number of ways to love God. Throughout the Bible there are multiple illustrations, from the Ten Commandments (Exodus 20:1-17) to Jesus' Sermon on the Mount (Matthew 5–7). These God-centered actions include acknowledging that there is only one God and not multiple gods like money, career, and sex. We are not to misuse the name of God by cursing. A major way of loving God is to keep a day of rest, sometimes called a "sabbath." The sabbath was originally the seventh day of the week, the day on which God rested after creating the universe. Jews consider the sabbath to be from sundown on Friday to sundown on Saturday. Most Christians celebrate Jesus' rising from the dead on the first day of the week by keeping the first day, Sunday, as a sabbath. On this day of rest, we read our Bibles to hear God speaking to us, pray so that we may speak with God, talk with family members and friends, gather with other Christians, refrain from everyday work, and generally refocus ourselves to pay attention to God. In our society, so intent on "busy-ness," the simple yet hard act of pulling back and redirecting our sight one day a week is a profound way of experiencing a good life.

Jesus himself provided for us one more example of loving God profoundly. On the night before his death, Jesus went to a garden to pray. Jesus recognized that he had offended the religious and political officials and that his arrest and possible death were imminent. Jesus knelt in prayer and asked God not to have him face death; he said, "Remove this cup from me" (Luke 22:42). In essence, Jesus said, "Give me my life; don't put me to death." But Jesus also said, "Yet, not my will but yours be done" (Luke 22:42), or "Nevertheless, I'll do what you want me to do." Jesus' life revolved around God, not the other way around.

Oscar Arnulfo Romero was also willing to put God first. He was reared and educated in San Salvador and in his first career was a carpenter. He then returned to school to become a Roman Catholic priest and quickly rose within the ranks of the priesthood. Shortly after being appointed an archbishop in 1977, however, two priest-friends were assassinated by right-wing death squads of the military dictatorship in El Salvador, the country in which they were serving. He condemned his own government, spoke out for the poor, stood up for human rights, criticized the United States for its support of a military dictatorship, and challenged the Roman Catholic Church to stand with his nation's oppressed people. He once said, "My life has been threatened many times. I have to confess that as a Christian I do not believe in death without resurrection. If they kill me, I will rise again in the Salvadoran people. I will feel him [Jesus] close when I offer him my last breath. More important than the moment of death is giving him all of life and living for him." During a worship service, in which the Scripture was John 12:24—"Unless a grain of wheat falls into the earth and dies, it remains just a single grain; but if it dies, it bears much fruit"—Romero was killed as he lifted up the cup of Holy Communion.

LOVE YOUR NEIGHBOR

Just as important as the first commandment—love God—is a second principle of good living that Jesus offers us: love other people.

Jesus showed us how to care for other people by a dramatic act of foot-washing. Jesus and his friends had been traveling all day to Jerusalem from an outlying town. In those days everyone wore sandals, not socks and shoes.

When it came time for supper, it was customary for a servant or a slave to take a bowl of water and wash off the feet of the people who came for the meal. At this meal, however, Jesus got down on his knees, tied a towel around his waist, took a basin of water, washed off the feet of his friends, and then dried their feet. Jesus' friends were appalled. Foot-washing was the task for a servant, not a master. Yet Jesus said, "I give you a new commandment, that you love one another. Just as I have loved you, you also should love one another" (John 13:34). Some congregations re-enact this event every year during the week before Easter.

Millard Fuller understood this self-giving love. Fuller was a lawyer and businessman who became a millionaire by the age of twenty-nine. As his professional work prospered, Fuller's relationship with his wife and children began to deteriorate, however. Hearing a call by Jesus Christ in 1966, the Fullers began to sell their possessions and to search for a new way to put love into action. Two years into their journey, they traveled to Koinonia Farms, a multiracial community in south Georgia. While there, the leader of Koinoia Farms, Clarence Jordan, said to Fuller that what the poor need is not charity but capital, not caseworkers but coworkers. And what the rich need is a wise, honorable, and just way of divesting themselves of their overabundance. Fuller discovered that if we are to be reborn, we must completely change our ways. The Fullers began to build small homes on a no-profit, no-interest basis, practicing the "economics of Jesus." Today, over one million people throughout the United States and around the world now live in more than 250,000 Habitat for Humanity homes.

We cannot, however, love other people until we first love ourselves. If God created each one of us and called each one of us good, each one of us is worthy of loving ourselves. One way we can love ourselves is by caring for our own selves as much as God cares for us. In their personal lifestyles, Christians strive to avoid anything that hurts them. For example, loving ourselves may include not using alcohol and other drugs inappropriately, avoiding overeating, and ending destructive relationships. We care for our bodies because we are God's special creation (1 Corinthians 3:16). Finally, caring for ourselves includes getting some exercise, nurturing our minds, going to the dentist, and seeing our doctor when we have need.

This self-love must then extend in growing circles to other people. One of the New Testament writers told other Christians, "If a brother or sister is naked and lacks daily food, and one of you says to them, 'Go in peace; keep warm and eat your fill,' and yet you do not supply their bodily needs, what is the good of that? . . . You see that a person is justified by works and not by faith alone. . . . Faith without works is . . . dead" (James 2:15-16, 24, 26). What does this message mean for us? When we see someone stranded by the side of the road, we stop and help. When a cashier gives us an extra $20.00 by mistake, we return the money. When a vendor to our company offers us a gift on the side, we refuse. When we log onto our computer at work, we do not scan for pornography or plan our family's vacation; we work. At work and at home we must not lie and cheat. In our relationships with other people, gossiping and quarreling are not allowed. In our relationships with other Christians, we are expected to trust one another and to offer assistance whenever it is needed.

Even deeper, the Christian life is a life of justice for all people. Jesus' own ministry began with these words:

> The Spirit of the Lord is upon me,
>   because [God] has anointed me
>   to bring good news to the poor.
> [God] has sent me to proclaim release
>   to the captives
>   and recovery of sight to the blind,
>   to let the oppressed go free.
>
> (Luke 4:18)

Christians are expected to give generously of our time, talents, and financial resources to congregations and charities that care for our neighbors. We share with people who are hungry, naked, strangers, and in prison. We tell the truth to people in power, and we work for peace. We avoid polluting God's creation.

Born in Atlanta, Georgia in 1929, the son of a Baptist preacher, Martin Luther King, Jr., understood the linkage between Christianity and social action. After ordination as a Baptist preacher and completion of his Ph.D. in theology, King began to preach at Dexter Avenue Baptist Church in Montgomery, Alabama. At first King preferred to concentrate on his studies and congregation, but other African-American pastors in the community insisted that he become their leader. Rejecting anyone with the veneer of religion who segregated persons on the basis of the color of their skin, his goal was to integrate people not only with God but also with one another and with themselves. He understood his movement as putting Christianity into action. Influenced by Mohandas Gandhi, the leader of nonviolent resistance to British control over India, King taught active nonviolence as the means for racial reconciliation in this country. Later he opposed the Vietnam War and injustice around the world. Throughout his work, however, King always used Christian images and biblical language to challenge everyone, and especially Christians, to seek justice.

This perspective of loving justice begins to answer the question of whether Christians should be socially active and engaged in politics. How does being a disciple of Jesus Christ affect one's views and behavior regarding business ethics, political morality, and international affairs? Being Christian means being involved throughout the world and in every institution in our world. The result of human sin is not just what an individual sin does to individual persons; sin also distorts all of our social relationships. Slavery, the oppression of women and persons of color, the rejection of people who live different kinds of lives, poverty, war, and environmental destruction are all signs of sin. God calls Christians to overcome these sins in our world through our words, our actions, and our votes. Loving one's neighbor means being involved in food banks, housing projects, walks against hunger, opposition to gambling, work for international peace and justice, political elections, and collections for the poor. God also calls us to ask why people are hungry, homeless, in prison, and at war around the world. When God starts working in us and through us to be loving toward other people, everything is on the table.

"Christianity is an invitation to be part of an alien people who make a difference because they see something that cannot otherwise be seen without Christ...the creation of a new people who have aligned themselves with the seismic shift that has occurred in the world since Christ."
Stanley Hauerwas and William Willimon

HOW TO BEGIN BEING GOOD

So where do you start? How do you begin? Following Jesus Christ, loving God, and loving our neighbor seems almost impossible. The good news is that living such a good life is not something we achieve but rather is a gift that is given to us by God through the Holy Spirit. Following Jesus Christ in love is not a work we do but a generous gift to us from God. To be like Jesus requires that we receive the gift of the Holy Spirit, knowing that "God's love has been poured into our hearts through the Holy Spirit" (Romans 5:5). Having received the gift of the Holy Spirit, we must then bear fruit worthy of the Spirit. As Jesus said, "I am the vine, you are the branches. Those who abide in me and I in them bear much fruit" (John 15:5). Doing good is not something we do to deserve God's love; keeping God's laws reflects the fact that we have already received God's love.

Following Jesus Christ by loving God and other people is a way of living in which we always try to discern what God is asking us to do as we continue our spiritual journey. We begin by trying. If we do not want the results, we will not pay the price. If we do not want to lose weight, we will not lose a pound. The songwriter in the Bible knew about the desire to have a good life when he wrote,

Create in me a clean heart, O God,
    and put a new and right spirit within me.
Do not cast me away from your presence,
    and do not take your holy spirit from me.
Restore to me the joy of your salvation,
    and sustain in me a willing spirit.

(Psalm 51:10-12)

The first step, which is the hardest step, God has already begun in us: the recognition of how far we have yet to go. Once that has happened, our eyes, hearts, ears, and hands can begin to move in Christlike ways.

"My faith demands...that I do whatever I can, wherever I can, wherever I can, for as long as I can with whatever I have to try to make a difference."   *Jimmy Carter*

Being good ultimately means being attentive to God's presence in our life and developing our relationship with Jesus Christ in every way. Have you experienced a first true love? You saw a face, and maybe a body, that you liked and you said hello. If there was a spark, you talked a little while and maybe went on a date. As the relationship continued, you shared common experiences; and the more you were together, the closer you became. You started "seeing each other." The more you discovered about each other, the closer you became. Soon you cared just as much about the other person as you cared about yourself. The other's happiness became your happiness. So it is with your relationship with Jesus Christ.

BLESSINGS OF A GOOD LIFE

What is the result of following Jesus Christ by loving God and our neighbors? We do not become good to prove to Jesus Christ that we are worthy of God's love; Jesus Christ loved us before we loved him. Jesus Christ does not love us any more when we are good; he loved us when we did none of these good things. Rather, as we follow Jesus Christ and reflect his love, our way of living changes our lives and the lives of everyone around us. Paul speaks of these positive changes as a bountiful harvest of the fruits of the Spirit-filled life: "The fruit of the Spirit is love, joy, peace, patience, kindness, generosity, faithfulness, gentleness, and self-control" (Galatians 5:22-23a). Are not these qualities much greater than being happy?

> "Do all the good you can, by all the means you can, in all the ways you can, in all the places you can, to all the people you can, as long as you can."
>
> John Wesley, adapted

Eleven

WHY SHOULD I JOIN ANY GROUP THAT WILL HAVE ME AS A MEMBER?

Choice is a powerful human tool. Perhaps the most powerful there is. And the beauty of it is, it's available to everyone.

Stephen Bauman

There are different kinds of gifts, but the same Spirit [distributes them]. There are different kinds of service, but the same Lord. There are different kinds of working, but the same God works all of them in all [people].

Now to each one the manifestation of the Spirit is given for the common good. To one there is given . . . the message of wisdom, to another the message of knowledge . . . to another gifts of healing . . . to another miraculous powers. . . . All these are the work of one and the same Spirit, and [the Spirit] gives them to each one, just as [the Spirit] determines.

The body is a unit, though it is made up of many parts; and though all its parts are many, they form one body. So it is with Christ. For we were all baptized by one Spirit into one body— whether Jews or Greeks, slave or free. . . .

Now . . . if the foot should say, "Because I am not a hand, I do not belong to the body," it would not for that reason cease to be part of the body. And if the ear should say, "Because I am not an eye, I do not belong to the body," it would not for that reason cease to be part of the body. If the whole body were an eye, where would the sense of hearing be? . . . But in fact God has arranged the parts in the body, every one of them, just as [God] wanted them to be. . . . As it is, there are many parts, but one body.

The eye cannot say to the hand, "I don't need you!" And the head cannot say to the feet, "I don't need you!" On the contrary, those parts of the body that seem to be weaker are indispensable, and the parts that we think are less honorable we treat with special honor. . . . But God has combined the members of the body together and has given greater honor to the parts that lacked it, so that there should be no division in the body, but that its parts should have equal concern for each other. If one part suffers, every part suffers with it; if one part is honored, every part rejoices with it.

Now you are the body of Christ, and each one of you is a part of it. (1 Corinthians 12:4-27 NIV)

In J. R .R. Tolkien's *Lord of the Rings* trilogy, Frodo Baggins, a hobbit, embarks on a dangerous journey to the Dark Mountain. The only way Frodo will succeed in his journey is with the assistance of some very good, and very strange, friends. There is Gandalf the wizard; fellow hobbits Sam, Pippin, and Merry; Legolas the elf; Gimli the dwarf; and even two humans, Boromir and Aragorn. While it was vital that Frodo be strong, wise, and brave, evil was defeated only because of the collective strength, wisdom, bravery, and even the sacrifice of life of Frodo's companions on the journey. Frodo's story is an old story of achieving a larger task by being in community with other people. Remember Dorothy in *The Wizard of Oz*? Dorothy could never have gotten to the Emerald City without the Scarecrow, Tin Man, and Cowardly Lion. The Tour de France, a company objective, the Super Bowl, the Little League World Series, a neighborhood project, and NASCAR auto races are always achieved or won by companions working together.

After Jesus' resurrection and rising into heaven, God created the Church in Jerusalem (Acts 2). On a day we call Pentecost, the Holy Spirit blew on the followers of Jesus. Like God blowing the breath of life into people at creation, God blew a new creative breath and formed a new people. The followers of Jesus began to speak in every language, and people from around the world heard about Jesus in their own tongue. On that day three thousand people decided to follow Jesus Christ. These new followers believed in Jesus Christ, shared their worldly belongings with one another, gave away their possessions to people in need, studied together, and worshiped together. They learned that by denying themselves, putting God first, and joining together, they found the meaning of life. The Church of Jesus Christ continued to grow and is still growing today. Over two billion people around the world, about a third of the world's population, are Christians.

That was the early church, but none of us has experienced a congregation just like that. Many of our experiences with organized congregations have been rather different. Some of us may remember going to a different worship service. The sanctuary was dark and cold. The organ music was slow. The preacher would never stop talking. The people seemed stern and serious. Who would want to go to a congregation like that?

Where did we get this church that's so prim and proper. Anybody who reads the New Testament will discover a Jesus who loved to party with all kinds of people. The publicans and "sinners" loved him because he partied with them. The lepers of society found in him someone who would eat and drink with them. And while the solemnly pious could not relate to what he was about, those lonely people who usually didn't get invited to parties took to him with excitement.

For the past two thousand years, the Church (capitalized to indicate its universal aspect) has been a place of strong disagreements and even wars. We lament that Christians have killed other Christians and believers of other faiths, especially Jews and Muslims, in the name of Jesus Christ.

In the present day, we also know congregations of people who are rude to outsiders, fight with one another, battle over money, and act one way on Sunday and another way on Monday. Why would anyone want to be involved with a group of people like that? As Groucho Marx, the comedian, is often quoted as asking, "Why would I want to join any group that would have somebody like me as a member?"

WHAT IS THE "CHURCH"?

What is the "Church"? Is the Church like the Civitans, the Red Cross, the Masons, an Internet chat room, a coffee house, or a credit union? Is the Church the Sunday worship service? Is the Church a building filled with Christian symbols like the cross? Is the Church the pastor, priest, or minister, often wearing strange robes and using strange words? Is the Church a particular brand of Christianity: Baptist, Roman Catholic, Lutheran, Syrian Orthodox, Presbyterian, United Church of Canada, United Church of Christ, or United Methodist?

The answer is simple. The Church is the gathering of people who follow Jesus Christ and are inspired by the Holy Spirit to live in community with one another.

The word *Church* means "a community that is called together." God through the Holy Spirit calls followers of Jesus Christ out of their individualistic, self-centered lives to be in fellowship with other people who follow Jesus Christ. As Paul wrote in the New Testament, "You are citizens with the saints and also members of the household of God" (Ephesians 2:19).

In addition to being a new community of people, even more so, the Church is Christ's body. This new body is not a fixed institution; as Paul described it, the Church is a growing and moving organism. This body consists of Jesus Christ, who is the head, and members, who are the parts of the body: eyes, ears, legs, arms, and heart. Individual congregations are just one part of the Church universal. As the Church, we are not an organization or a club or a business, we are an organism that is Spirit-filled and Spirit-guided!

> *"God has called us into being as a community and our life as a community, though fraught with struggles and failures, is a powerful act of revelation, testimony and service."*
>
> *Society of Saint John the Evangelist*

The first step in being a Christian demands a commitment to Jesus Christ as Guide. Jesus Christ calls each of us as an individual to "follow me" (Matthew 4:19).

This personal commitment to follow, however, is but a first step in the Christian journey. When we follow Jesus Christ and declare him to be our companion, this commitment takes place within a community of people who also believe that Jesus Christ is our Savior. A Christian is a transformed person who lives in a transformed community. Jesus Christ calls each of us to be one—but not the only one—of his disciples.

Not every Christian has always shared this view of living in community. In the fifth century in the land of Syria, there lived a holy man called Simon. Although he was a hermit, living alone in the desert, he occasionally saw and visited with other Christian hermits. When Simon was about thirty years old, he decided to take his solitary life, literally, to another level. He began to live on a small platform on top of a pillar. This strange contraption would isolate him from everyone and everything, sort of like some media hosts who camp out until their ball team wins a game or money is raised for a charity. Over the years Simon kept raising his pillar until it was sixty feet tall. Simon lived on his small platform for thirty-six years. Because of his spiritual discipline of isolation, he became known as Saint Simon of the Pillar. Today, some Christians still isolate themselves from the world by living in remote places or cocooning themselves from the world. Fundamentally, however, Christians cannot live isolated lives.

Being part of an organized congregation is also a necessary step in following Jesus Christ. A Christian without a congregational family is a contradiction. A solitary Christian is like a child without parents, a quarterback without a team, a bee without a hive, a fish without a school, a bird without a flock, or a cow without a herd. An African proverb says it well: "Two antelope walk together so that one can blow the dust from the other's eye." The New Testament declares that the collective body of the followers of Jesus Christ "are a chosen race, a royal priesthood, a holy nation, God's own people." The Bible continues, "once you were not a people, but now you are God's people" (1 Peter 2:9-10). In other words, an individual may choose to be a soccer player; but by virtue of being a soccer player, the player must also be part of a team. The church provides the relationships, structures, and practices to help an individual grow in a relationship with Jesus Christ. The Church is God's visible and active answer to a broken, hurting, alienated, and destructive world.

THE MISSION OF THE CHURCH: SHARING THE GOOD NEWS

Responding to the hurting needs of everyone, the Church has one primary mission, given to it by Jesus Christ: "Go therefore and make disciples of all nations, baptizing them in the name of the Father and of the Son and of the Holy Spirit, and teaching them to obey everything that I have commanded you" (Matthew 28:19-20). The number-one reason the Church exists is to invite other women, men, youth, and children to follow Jesus Christ. Congregations fulfill this responsibility through programs and ministries and through members telling other people about Jesus Christ by their words and their actions.

Many persons have started following Jesus Christ through their own experience with the Church. John Wesley was a lifelong Christian who had strengthened his relationship with Jesus Christ within the Church. Wesley grew up in the Church of England, was baptized by his pastor father, was confirmed at age ten, and even became a priest in the Church of England. His whole life was spent within the body of Christ. Then, during a small-group meeting with other Christians, Wesley experienced an intense experience with Jesus Christ.

As Wesley wrote, "In the evening I went very unwillingly to a society at Aldersgate Street [in London], where one was reading Luther's Preface to the Epistle to the Romans. About a quarter before nine, while Luther was describing the change which God works in the heart through faith in Christ, I felt my heart strangely warmed. I felt I did trust in Christ, Christ alone for salvation; and an assurance was given me that Christ had taken away my sins, even *mine*, and saved *me* from the law of sin and death."

After this experience Wesley affirmed the role of being in community by organizing small groups of disciplined Christians who then formed Methodist communities throughout the world for Bible study, prayer, and social witness.

As a living organism of disciples committed to Jesus Christ, the Church possesses three unique ways of sharing the good news about Jesus Christ: being a faithful body of people, preaching the Bible, and celebrating the sacraments.

1. A FAITHFUL COMMUNITY

The first way that the Church shares its mission is by being a place of fellowship: a community of people who work together to serve God. In Christianity, people hold one another accountable to put God first in their lives. Sometimes this work of being faithful followers is difficult. Especially when a member of a congregation fails or hurts someone or violates boundaries or acts as a hypocrite, the gathered community must set the right direction for everyone to follow. The Church is a community of followers of Jesus Christ who dream and get frustrated, love their families one day and scream at them the next, hug and fight, and give generously and then act stingily. All of these people, however, share a common passion: to love God and other people passionately.

Being in a fellowship community is a major benefit of being a Church member. As the Church, Christians become a family to one another. The Bible declares that members should "have unity of spirit, sympathy, love for one another, a tender heart, and a humble mind" (1 Peter 3:8). In the Church, we watch over one another with love and care. When a child is born or a parent dies, when a marriage begins or a marriage ends, when life is good and when life collapses, members hold up one another. When we travel to a strange town or even to another part of the world, we can always find sisters and brothers in local congregations. The Church operates not on the basis of rules but on the basis of relationships in which we uphold one another and accomplish more together than anyone could accomplish alone.

2. SHARING THE WORD OF GOD

The second way the Church shares its good news is by preaching the Word of God, proclaiming Jesus Christ as presented to us through the Bible. We believe that the Bible becomes a living word when faithful people proclaim Jesus Christ. While people may hear about some of the teachings of Jesus through television, magazines, the Internet, and friends, only the Church tells about the work of Jesus Christ day after day, week after week, year after year. By reading the Bible and then preaching and teaching about how Jesus Christ speaks to our contemporary lives, the Church spreads the good news about Jesus Christ.

As the Church shares God's stories, a second benefit of Church membership becomes obvious: personal growth. When we commune with God through preaching and worship, our relationship with Jesus Christ grows stronger. In the Church we discover more about ourselves, unleash new talents, serve our communities in new ways, receive affirmation, are encouraged to do better, and know that we are never alone. As Paul said, "we must grow up in every way into . . . Christ" (Ephesians 4:15).

3. BAPTISM AND HOLY COMMUNION

Baptism and Holy Communion are the third unique way the Church tells other people the good news. In the Protestant tradition, we affirm two sacraments, two special activities instituted by Jesus Christ that reveal him to us. In Baptism and Holy Communion, God's love is made visible through a specific activity by the whole company of Christians.

In Baptism, through water and the Holy Spirit the Church welcomes children, youth, and adults into the body of Christ. The Ethiopian official, when he heard the news about Jesus, asked Philip to baptize him. No one is born with membership in the Church. The Church alone adopts us into the living community by washing us clean and giving us new life. In the ritual of Baptism, the Church proclaims the grace of God, asks the persons being baptized if they believe in Jesus Christ as Savior, professes the historic beliefs of the Church, gives thanks over water, and washes the persons by pouring or sprinkling water on their head or by immersing them in water. Through Baptism, we remember that we do not choose to belong to the Church; rather, God in the Church through Baptism incorporates us into the body of Christ. Christians in every age, in every place, and in every time, from Baptists to Russian Orthodox to Pentecostals to Lutherans to Presbyterians to United Methodists, are part of the living body of Christ through Baptism. The universal quality of Baptism is why every member of every local congregation is a part of the worldwide Church.

Through Holy Communion, the Church invites everyone to share in the Lord's Supper, the holy meal of bread and wine or grape juice. The name "Holy Communion" declares that in this meal we experience communion in a special way with Jesus Christ and the gathered people. Through taking the bread and cup, blessing the elements, breaking the bread, and giving the bread and cup, we experience Jesus Christ in the meal. The broken bread and the shared cup remind us that Jesus' love was so great that he was willing to be broken on a cross and shed his blood for everyone. The meal also reminds us that after his resurrection, Jesus made himself known to two of his first followers, as we discussed in chapter 4, through the breaking of bread at the meal he shared with them at Emmaus (Luke 24:13-31). Holy Communion is the family meal at which Jesus Christ is the host, and everyone is invited to receive. When we receive the bread and the cup, we are in communion with God and all Christians everywhere.

Through the sacraments in particular, we discover a third major benefit of Church membership: communion with God. As the first followers of Jesus "devoted themselves to the apostles' teaching and fellowship, to the breaking of bread and the prayers" (Acts 2:42), so Church members do the same today to discover Jesus Christ. While Jesus Christ can commune with us at the beach or on top of a mountain, it is especially in the sacraments that we intentionally open ourselves to feel and taste the presence of God.

WHY BELONG?

Many North Americans today are reluctant to join any organization, especially the Church. People do not trust any organized group, from bowling leagues to political parties to civic groups to professional organizations. People have too little time to give, are frightened by the possibility of close relationships, and have fears about the financial cost. Many people are comfortable not being part of any organization.

Therefore, you may ask, even as you learn more about the basics of Christianity, "Can't I be a Christian without being a part of a local congregation? Can't I follow Jesus Christ without associating with hypocritical Christians?" The simple answer is that belonging contributes to personal growth and to the good of our society. Each congregation of the Church universal provides worship every week, year after year. In addition, congregations offer learning opportunities through Bible studies, Sunday school classes, and special ministries with children and youth. Opportunities to serve, from cooking in soup kitchens to building homes for the poor to traveling overseas to assisting in emergencies in the community, are also ministries of the Church. All these opportunities are necessary for each of us to continue in our journeys. But personal growth alone is not enough of a reason to join; Church members also care for our society at large.

Despite the Church's many past and current social failures, the Church has been a leader in the fight against slavery, built hospitals, started schools and colleges, worked to end child labor, sought racial justice, cared for the environment, worked against world hunger, and helped raise the hope of peace. If you want to make a difference in your own life and in the lives of people around you, there is no better place to start than the Church.

SOME QUESTIONS

Is the Church only for good people, or is it also for people like us with mixed stories? The Church has often debated this issue: is the Church a safe refuge for perfect people, or is it a hospital for sick people? Every time people inside the Church believe themselves to be better than people outside the church, God reminds us that the body of Christ is a safe haven to which broken and imperfect persons can come and be made whole. If the Church were restricted to perfect people, every congregational building would be empty. The Church—even when Spirit-filled, full of faithful disciples, honestly preaching God's Word, and sharing the sacraments—is full of human beings affected by the power of sin. Hypocrites abound. But with Jesus Christ as our head, guide, and companion, the Church points us in the right direction.

Do we expect all the people in the church to think and act just like one another? Because no two Christians are ever the same, the Church is and should be a very diverse place. At their best, all congregations are filled with women and men, young and old, people of every color in the rainbow, and maybe even a few saints among the bountiful sinners. As the Bible says, "We were all baptized into one body—Jews or Greeks, slaves or free" (1 Corinthians 12:13). The Church has no interest in making everyone like any one person or like anyone else. Every person is a unique creation of God. No two persons ever think or act in exactly the same way. The Church at its best encourages everyone to use their diverse personalities and talents to the greater glory of the whole body.

What is the purpose of ministers and pastors? In the Church, filled with followers of Jesus Christ, every member is a minister. Now, considering every person to be a minister may be a new concept for you. Aren't ministers supposed to be the holy people who tell everyone else what they should do? Some people believe the old adage, "Clergy are paid to be good; members are good for nothing." Pastors, priests, clergy, ordained ministers, church staff, and church leaders are in congregations to help give birth to the ministries of the Church. They are mentors for those who want to live faithfully. As they teach, preach, encourage, organize, challenge, comfort, and celebrate the sacraments, these women and men act as guides to the ministry of all the people. Pastors and church professionals are the persons who push us a little harder, who ask a little more of us, and who encourage us to go beyond what we believe are our limits. They pat us on the back when we do well. They challenge us when we do less than our best. They set goals for us that exceed our own private expectations. These professional church people have been called and trained and have the experience necessary to encourage everyone.

But, guided by these leaders, every person in every congregation is called by Jesus Christ to be a minister. Members of a congregation teach Sunday school, sing in the choir, repair the physical facilities, raise the money, go on youth retreats, repair homes, give food to the poor, pray for other people, visit friends who are sick, type the newsletter, and perform all the countless other activities of a Christian community. Everyone is responsible for the total ministry of a congregation.

WHAT DOES THE CHURCH EXPECT?

If you are considering belonging, we want to be honest about the Church's expectations. There is a difference between an "attender" and a "member." An "attender" is a volunteer who drops by for worship, Bible study, family activities, and support in times of need. An "attender" is a consumer of a congregation's activities. On the other hand, a "member" is a disciple who comes for worship, Bible study, family activities, and support in times of need but is also committed to serve other people when other people come to worship, study Scripture, participate in activities, and ask for help in times of need. A "member" is both a consumer and a service provider. Each member of the Church must be a living part of the body of Jesus Christ.

When people join a local congregation of the Church universal, they are typically asked a series of questions. In addition to questions about their relationship with Jesus Christ, these persons are also asked either specifically or in general to be active members of a local congregation. These questions related to membership often include the following:

1. Will you uphold the Church with prayer? All members are asked to pray consistently for their own congregation and for all Christians everywhere (1 Thessalonians 1:1-2).

2. Will you support the Church with your presence? Being a member means being present with other members during weekly worship, at small-group gatherings, at social occasions, on mission projects, and when a member has a crisis (Hebrews 10:24-25).

3. Will you contribute financial gifts to the Church? The Church depends on the monetary gifts of each individual member (Ezra 3:7; Mark 12:41-44). People are asked to give sacrificially, as Jesus gave himself totally to us. The Church and all local congregations need money to provide worship, to teach the children, to pay the utility bills, to support the staff, to be in mission, and through all of these ministries to serve one another and the whole world.

4. Will you strengthen the Church with your service? The Church needs talented people who willingly share their skills with the whole body (1 Peter 4:10). Some persons can teach, others can build houses, some can keep the nursery, others can cook, some can clean floors, others can share their stories with other people, some can sing in the choir—the list goes on and on.

Church membership is a serious commitment. Compare it to this little story. Some farm animals were talking about the upcoming breakfast fundraiser for the farmer's local congregation. The cow declared that she was going to donate milk. The chicken was pleased that she had been asked to donate eggs. When the pig arose to speak, she thanked everyone for their donation but mentioned that her gift would require total commitment; the pig was offering bacon and sausage. The Church needs fewer cows and chickens and more pigs.

BEING PART OF THE BODY

Why should you consider being a member of Christ's body? Why be a member of a congregation that would love to have you as a fellow disciple of Jesus Christ? Consider the following two stories:

At Special Olympics, women and men with handicapping conditions compete against one another for gold, silver, and bronze medals. Just like in the regular Olympics, and sometimes in real life, there can be only one winner. Well, there was a running competition for men. When the gun sounded, all the runners took off as fast as they could run. Now, not every runner was able to run well. Some runners were on crutches, others wore artificial legs, a few had no arms, and a couple of runners were mentally challenged. Suddenly, one runner stumbled and then fell down. He toppled over, then sat up, held his leg, and just sat there on the track. All the runners stopped running. One by one they turned around and returned to the injured runner. The competitors then helped the injured runner up and carried him to the finish line. Each of the competitors received a medal. At its best, this is the Church that would love to have you as a member.

In 2002, nine miners were trapped for five days in the Quecreek Mine in western Pennsylvania. When the mine collapsed, the nine men escaped through a four-foot high shaft with water up to their shoulders. The men hoped that help would come, but their only source of strength was one another.

The men tied themselves together with a plastic-coated steel cable; if they died they would be found together. As they sat in the dark, fighting the cold and low-oxygen air, they sat back-to-back for warmth. If someone began shaking from the cold, the others would sandwich the cold one between them. They told jokes and fantasized about their favorite foods. They found a lunch pail with one corned-beef sandwich and a soft drink, which they all shared.

On the fifth day, the miners were saved. They survived by leading, holding up, feeding, encouraging, and tying themselves to one another. Their example is also how Christians live as the Church of Jesus Christ.

Twelve

SHARING THE EXPERIENCE

Before us it is blessed, behind us it is blessed,
  below us it is blessed, above us it is blessed,
    around us it is blessed as we set out with Christ.
Our speech is blessed as we set out for God.
  With beauty before us, with beauty behind us,
    with beauty below us, with beauty above us,
  with beauty around us,
    we set out for a holy place indeed.

Traditional Navajo Prayer

Do you remember the story about the inquiring Nicodemus who came to Jesus at night? What about the woman at the well looking for a drink of water? Zacchaeus up the tree waiting to see Jesus? The scared disciples on the road to Emmaus? Moses in front of the burning bush? Philip and the Ethiopian official in a chariot discussing the Bible? The runaway son trying to figure out what to say to his father? The woman caught in adultery and ready to be killed? The bleeding woman looking for healing? Jesus teaching his friends to pray? The lawyer asking Jesus how to live a good life? Paul's illustration about the Church as the body of Christ?

We began with Nicodemus, a man who came seeking Jesus at night. We end with the story of Mary Magdalene, a woman who came seeking Jesus in the darkness before dawn (John 20:1-18). It was the third day since Jesus' death. The Gospels of Mark and Luke tell us that Mary Magdalene was accompanied by other women and that they went to Jesus' tomb to cover his body with spices, a sign of respect and honor. In John's Gospel, when Mary arrived, the tomb was empty. She ran to Peter and another disciple, who came and saw the empty tomb and the linen wrappings that had been on Jesus' body. They did not understand what had happened. The men returned home, and Mary remained weeping outside the tomb. Once again, she looked into the tomb; and this time she saw two angels. They asked her why she was weeping. When she told them, "They have taken away my Lord, and I do not know where they have laid him," she turned around and a man she assumed to be a gardener greeted her by name. It was Jesus, risen from the dead! Mary came seeking Jesus, but he was already there waiting for her! We remember on this day a central theme of Christianity: Before we seek God, God is seeking us.

One of the Bible's songs includes this verse:

I will call to mind the deeds of the Lord;
    I will remember your wonders of old.
I will meditate on all your work,
    and muse on your mighty deeds.

(Psalm 77:11-12)

FEAR OF FORGETTING

You may soon forget many of the specifics of what you have read, but we hope that you have learned about the

Christian faith. Unfortunately it may be easy to forget—to return to your daily rituals and forget your new insights, neglect your new intentions, and forget who you are and who God is as you continue your journey of life.

THE JOY OF REMEMBERING

The alternative to forgetting is remembering. Do you remember your initial hunger for God? Do you remember the stories from the Bible? Do you remember the prayers? When we remember, we do not just live in the past, reminiscing about past experiences. Good memories revive in us both energy and power; we relive those experiences.

Yet, we cannot live in the past. Men and women who live only in the past have no present and no future. They are doomed to live in the past. Sharing and being intentional about the next steps are ways to move ahead in your journey.

THE GIFT OF SHARING

One of our most basic human needs is to share our experiences with other people. When we meet a famous person, we tell everyone. When we catch a big fish, the fish gets bigger every time we tell the story. When we get a raise, we want to yell out loud. This need to share is why we invite friends to celebrate our birthday or an anniversary.

The story about Jesus and the woman at the well is one model of how we might share our experiences. When Jesus came to the well to drink, the woman came to draw water up out of the well, and Jesus asked her for a drink of water. After a conversation, the woman realized that

Jesus was the guide she had always been expecting. The woman left her water jar, went back into her city, and told everyone that she had met the Savior. Then everyone left the city and went out to meet Jesus (John 4:1-30). One woman discovered Jesus and told other people, and they, too, became his followers.

We now exist in an in-between time. We are living in the time and place between the beginning of our lives and the end, between never knowing Jesus Christ and waiting to greet him at the conclusion of history.

We encourage you in the days to come to share your experiences of your spiritual journey with other people. Such sharing can be frightening. Too many people have negative experiences of people witnessing about their Christian journey. Some of us have had the experience of a stranger walking up to us on the street or in a mall and asking, "Are you a Christian?" That verbal confrontation is one way of telling one's story, but oftentimes this activity may be obnoxious.

Sharing your Christian journey, however, can be very natural. Faith-sharing is like when you go to a good restaurant or a great movie or when you fall in love: you cannot keep the experience to yourself. When a child is born, when a person has his or her first date, when a youth gets accepted into college, when a couple becomes engaged, we want to shout from the rooftop. When we have found something good, we cannot help sharing what we have found. This sharing of your journey with Jesus Christ can be done in a variety of ways.

SHARING BY ACTIONS

Sharing can begin by reflecting what you have discovered. As the moon reflects the sun, so we reflect the things that give light to our lives. If you are a fan of a sports team, you wear your team's colors. If you are a fan of the Green Bay Packers, you wear a large hunk of orange-foam cheese on your head. If you are the fan of an actress, you may wear your hair like she does or name your child after her. Because Christians believe that Jesus Christ has discovered us, we try to reflect him in our words, thoughts, and deeds.

"There are two ways of spreading light: to be the candle or the mirror that reflects it."   *Edith Wharton*

For example, when we attach ourselves to Jesus Christ, we begin to reflect him in our lives. If we know Jesus Christ is the Savior, we may wear a cross around our neck and act differently in every aspect of our lives. We follow Jesus Christ, love God, and love our neighbors. The old song is right: "They'll know we are Christians by our love." God's priorities become our priorities, and people begin to see Jesus Christ through us.

"We are going home to many who cannot read. So, Lord, make us Bibles so that those who cannot read the Book can read it in us."   *Prayer from China*

Living as a Christian makes a profound impact in the lives of other people. Acts of charity, kindness, justice, and righteousness win as many disciples of Jesus Christ as all the words in the world. When we donate to a charity, walk to fight hunger, pick up a piece of trash, refuse to gossip, walk a picket line, or write a letter to the editor, we witness about the God we follow.

SHARING WITH WORDS

Sharing our Christian journey also means telling people about Jesus Christ. Sharing Christian experiences is one beggar telling another beggar where to find food. It is not your responsibility to provide the food (God has provided a great feast). It is not your responsibility to make another person come to the feast (people must make up their own minds). It is not your responsibility "to save" anyone (that is up to God and the person). Sharing verbally simply requires that you tell the story of Jesus Christ through your words and then wait patiently for new relationships to develop between other people and God.

Here are some guidelines for sharing your journey with other people.

1. Begin with people you care about. While some people are comfortable sharing their Christian journey with strangers, most of us are not. The best people to share with are your family members, coworkers, friends, and neighbors. These people already know and trust you. They know you care about them and their journeys. When you direct your attention to people you love and care for, the Holy Spirit will give you all the power you need. Threats, obnoxious behaviors, and in-your-face confrontation are not consistent with sharing the good news of God's love. Likewise, you should not share your discoveries as a way to prop up the institutional church or to add a mark on the cover of your Bible or to prove what a good Christian you are. Just as shepherds look for lost sheep, as people look for a valuable treasure lost in their home, as parents look eagerly for lost children, so God has always been out looking for all God's children.

Sharing is simply you helping God by reminding other people that God is looking for them. We share because we care about someone else.

2. Choose the right occasion. Talk with the people over coffee, while driving in a car, while exercising at the Y, or while enjoying a ball game. Usually it does not work to call a friend on the phone and say, "I'm coming over to talk about Jesus Christ." Most of your friends will be gone by the time you arrive. But when you see a need in the lives of people you know—a parent dies, a job is lost, an illness comes, a big decision awaits, a marriage is in trouble—you will know it is the right time to share.

3. Start with people where they are. Every person is at a different place in her or his journey along the way. Begin by letting people describe to you their needs or desires. Listen carefully before you respond. Listen for hurts, anxieties, dreams, desires, and pains. Watch a person's body language when she or he speaks. Be quiet and listen.

4. Share; do not argue. Tell how you have experienced Jesus Christ. Tell about your relationship with him in your own words. Tell your story: what you have seen, what you have heard, how you felt, and how your life has changed. Explain that you know a God who came in the person of Jesus, who speaks to us through the Bible and with us in our prayers, who can forgive and make people whole, who points us to good lives, and who journeys with us every day. Do not point the finger at yourself; point the person to Jesus Christ. Do not try to force someone else to have the same experience you have had. When you tell your friends truthfully about your experiences, they will want to know more. Let the conversation take the time and space it needs; you do not need to tell everything the first time you share. When Jesus called his followers, they told their families and neighbors first; and thus Christianity began to grow.

5. Pray. At the end of the conversation, ask if you may say a short prayer or simply pray for the person later in the day. You do not need final answers or complete closure; you need to place your friend in the hands of Jesus Christ. For many people, a prayer with them may be the first time someone prayed directly for them. In simple, direct language, tell God the problem or the issue and ask for God's presence and guidance. Then say, "Amen." Sometimes this prayer may best come after the conversation has ended when you commend the other person to Jesus Christ.

Do not forget. Remember. Share through your actions. Share with your words. And as you remember and share, the journey with Jesus Christ continues, deepens, and moves ever onward and upward.

REFERENCES

INTRODUCTION

Lewis Carroll, *Alice's Adventures in Wonderland* (Random House, 1965), 71-72.

CHAPTER 1. So, Is This All There Is?

Anselm of Canterbury, "An Address" (Proslogion) in *A Scholastic Miscellany: Anselm to Ockham*, edited by Eugene R. Fairweather (Westminster Press, 1966), 73.

Augustine, *The Confessions of St. Augustine*, translated by E. B. Pusey (E. P. Dutton, 1951).

Albert Camus, quoted in "Conversations with Camus" by Howard Mumma in *The Best Spiritual Writing of 2001*, edited by Philip Zaleski (HarperCollins, 2001), 192.

William Leach, *A Country of Exiles: The Destruction of Place in American Life* (Pantheon, 1999).

John Marquand, *Point of No Return* (Academy Publishers, 1985).

Gabriel Garcia Marquez, *Love in the Time of Cholera* (Knopf, 1988; Everyman's Library, 1997), 199.

Henri J. M. Nouwen, *Reaching Out* (Doubleday, 1975), 65.

Walker Percy, *The Gramercy Winner* (unpublished novel in The Walker Percy Papers, The Southern Historical Collection, University of North Carolina).

CHAPTER 2. Who Is Jesus, and Why Should I Care?

Frederick Buechner, *The Hungering Dark* (Seabury Press, 1983), 66.

Thomas Cahill, *Desire of the Everlasting Hills: The World before and after Jesus* (Doubleday, 1999), 8.

Lois Cheney, *God Is No Fool* (Abingdon Press, 1969), 23.

C. S. Lewis, *The Joyful Christian* (Macmillan, 1977), 50-51.

Henri J. M. Nouwen, *The Road to Daybreak: A Spiritual Journey* (Doubleday, 1988), 150.

J. B. Phillips, *Good News* (Geoffrey Bles, 1964), 33-34.

CHAPTER 3. Why Am I Not Where I Want to Be?

Dante Alighieri, *Inferno*, translated by Mark Muse (Indiana University Press); lines 1-3.

Robert Fulghum, *Words I Wish I Wrote: A Collection of Writing That Inspired My Ideas* (HarperCollins, 1997), 159.

Carson McCullers, *The Collected Stories of Carson McCullers* (Houghton Mifflin, 1987), 2.

Thomas Merton, *Thoughts in Solitude* (Farrar, Straus and Giroux, 1956), 79.

John Ortberg, *Love Beyond Reason: Moving God's Love From Your Head to Your Heart* (Zondervan, 1988), 87.

Walker Percy, *Lost in the Cosmos: The Last Self-Help Book* (Farrar, Straus and Giroux, 1983), 9.

Cornelius Plantinga, *Not the Way It's Supposed to Be: A Breviary of Sin*, (Eerdmans, 1995), 84.

Simone Weil, *Gravity and Grace* (Routledge Classics, 1999), 88-89.

Charles Wesley, "He Breaks the Power of Canceled Sin," *The United Methodist Hymnal* (The United Methodist Publishing House, 1989), 57.

CHAPTER 4. What Happens When I Die?

Thomas Cahill, *The Desire of the Everlasting Hills: The World before and after Jesus* (Doubleday, 1999), 8.

Annie Dillard, *Pilgrim at Tinker Creek* (HarperCollins, 1988), 270.

C. S. Lewis, *Letters to Malcolm* (Harcourt, Brace and World, 1964), 93.

Rollo May, *My Quest for Beauty* (Saybrook, 1985), 60.

Richard John Neuhaus, "Born toward Dying," in *The Best Spiritual Writing 2000*, edited by Philip Zaleski (HarperCollins, 2000), 236.

Ninth Century Prayer, in *The United Methodist Hymnal* (The United Methodist Publishing House, 1989), 155.

Kathleen Norris, *Dakota: A Spiritual Geography* (Houghton Mifflin, 1993), 189.

Dorothy Sayers, *Introductory Papers on Dante* (Harper and Brothers, 1954), 66.

Bert O. States, "Death as a Ficticious Event," in *Hudson Review*. vol. 53, No. 3 (Autumn 2000), 424.

Desmond Tutu, quoted in *London Sunday Telegraph*, April 2001.

Thornton Wilder, *Our Town: A Play in Three Acts* (Coward McCann, 1938), 124-25.

Philip Yancey, *Reaching for the Invisible God: What Can We Expect to Find?* (Zondervan, 2000), 181.

Frances Young, *Face to Face: A Narrative Essay in the Theology of Suffering* (T & T Clark, 1990), 141-42.

CHAPTER 5. Can I Trust God?

Elizabeth Barrett Browning, *Aurora Leigh*, Seventh Book.

Frederick Buechner, *Wishful Thinking: A Seeker's ABC* (Harper-Collins, 1993), 119.

William Sloane Coffin, "Alex's Death," in *A Chorus of Witnesses: Model Sermons for Today's Preacher*, edited by Thomas G. Long and Cornelius Plantinga (Eerdmans, 1994), 262-66.

Barbara Kingsolver, *Small Wonder* (HarperCollins, 2002), 6.

Anne Lamott, *Bird by Bird: Some Instructions on Writing and Life*, (Random House, 1995), 30.

Kathleen Norris, *Amazing Grace: A Vocabulary of Faith* (Riverhead Books, 1998), 150-51.

Lisa Simpson, quoted in *The Gospel According to the Simpsons*, by Mark Pinsky (Westminster John Knox, 2001), 16.

Barbara Brown Taylor, *Mixed Blessings* (Cowley, 1998), 50.

Lauren Winner, *Girl Meets God: On the Path to a Spiritual Life* (Algonquin Books, 2002), 57.

CHAPTER 6. How Does God Speak to Me?

Augustine, *The Confessions*, translated by Maria Boulding (1997), 161-68.

Emil Brunner, *The Misunderstanding of the Church* (Lutterworth Press, 1953), 1.

Bruce Feiler, *Walking the Bible* (William Morrow, 2001), 11.

Richard Foster, *Celebration of Discipline* (HarperSanFrancisco, 1988).

John Killinger, *Beginning Prayer* (Upper Room Books, 1993), 16.

H. G. Wells, *A Short History of the World* (1922, Penguin Books, 2000), 22.

CHAPTER 7. If I Don't Feel Lost, Why Do I Need to Be Found?

Maya Angelou, interview on *Oprah Winfrey Show*, 2002.

William Campbell, *Brother to a Dragonfly* (Continuum, 1997).

Maxie Dunnam, *This Is Christianity* (Abingdon Press, 1994), 49.

Bob Dylan, "You Gotta Serve Somebody" on album *Slow Train Coming*, Columbia, 1979.

Ignatius of Loyola, *The Spiritual Exercises*, edited by David L. Fleming, Institute of Jesuit Sources, 1978, 105.

Pope John Paul II, *Pastoral Letter*. 23, April 2002, 1.

Kimberly Dunnam Reisman, *The Christ-Centered Woman* (Upper Room Books, 2000), 18.

She Wore a Yellow Ribbon, Argosy Pictures, 1949.

Pierre Teilhard de Chardin, *The Divine Milieu* (Harper & Row, 1960), 89.

CHAPTER 8. Can I Start Again?

Doris Donnelly, *Learning to Forgive* (Abingdon Press, 1979), 1.

Gerald Ford, quoted in "The Theology of Forgiveness," by Maya Mahs, *Time* magazine, September 23, 1974.

Georgia Harkness, *Understanding the Christian Faith* (Abingdon Press, 1947), 71.

Anne Lamott, *Traveling Mercies* (Pantheon Books, 1999), 3; 47-50.

Reynolds Price, *A Whole New Life* (Atheneum, 1994), 76.

Corrie ten Boom, *The Hiding Place* (Econo-Clad Books, 1999), 215.

Paul Tillich, *The Shaking of the Foundations* (Charles Scribner's Sons, 1948), 161.

James K. Wagner, *Blessed to Be a Blessing* (Upper Room, 1980), 28.

Terry Waite, quoted in *The Christian Life* by M .L. Lindvall (Geneva Press, 2001), 110.

CHAPTER 9. How Do I Speak to God?

Augustine, *The Confessions of St. Augustine*, translated by E. B. Pusey (E. P. Dutton, 1951).

John Calvin, *Corpus Reformatorum* 37, 402.

Cool Hand Luke, Jalem Productions, 1967.

Mohandas K. Gandhi, *Non-Violence in Peace and War*, Vol. 2 (Navajvan Publishing House, 1948), 77.

Rick Moody, "Why I Pray," first published in *Esquire*, October 1, 1997, published in *The Best Spiritual Writing 1998*, edited by Philip Zaleski (HarperSan Francisco, 1998).

James Mulholland, *Praying Like Jesus* (HarperSanFrancisco, 2001); front cover.

Mother Teresa, quoted in *A Life for God*, compiled by LaVonne Neff (Fount, 1997), 17-18.

Henri J. M. Nouwen, *The Genesee Diary* (Doubleday Image, 1981), 145.

Mark Twain, *The Adventures of Huckleberry Finn* (Heritage Press, 1884), chapter XXXI.

Evelyn Underhill, quoted in *The Life of Evelyn Underhill*, by Margaret Cropper (Kessenger Publishing, 2006), 106.

CHAPTER 10. How Can I Make a Life and Not Just a Living?

Prayer from Zaire heard by Andy Langford.

Jimmy Carter, quoted in *The Charlotte Observer*, October 21, 2002, 15a.

Habitat for Humanity website, www.habitat.org, accessed September 2008.

Stanley Hauerwas and William Willimon, *Resident Aliens* (Abingdon Press, 1985), 24.

Mother Teresa, quoted in Mother Teresa, by Ann Sebba (Doubleday, 1997), 46.

David G. Myers, *The American Paradox: Spiritual Hunger in an Age of Plenty* (Yale University Press, 2001), xi.

Oscar Arnulfo Romero, quoted in *Romero: A Life*, by James Brockman (Orbis Books, 1989), 248.

Rodney Stark, *The Rise of Christianity: How the Obscure, Marginal Jesus Movement Became the Dominant Religious Force in the Western World in a Few Centuries* (HarperCollins, 1997), 161.

CHAPTER 11. Why Should I Join Any Group That Will Have Me as a Member?

Stephen Bauman, *Simple Truths* (Abingdon Press, 2006), 65.

Society of Saint John the Evangelist, *The Rule of Life*, "The Witness of Life in Community."

John Wesley, in *The Bicentennial Edition of the Works of John Wesley*, Vol. 18, edited by Reginal Ward and Richard P. Heitzenrater (Abingdon, 1988), 249-50.

CHAPTER 12. Sharing the Experience

Prayer from China, in *The World at One in Prayer*, edited by D. J. Fleming (Harper, 1942), 43.

Traditional Navajo Prayer, in *600 Blessings and Prayer from Around the World* (Twenty-third Publications, 2001), 223.

Edith Wharton, "Vesalius in Zante," in *Artemis to Actaeon* (Norman Press, 2008).